Poking, Pinching & Pretending

Poking, Pinching

& Pretending

Documenting 'Toddlers' Explorations with Clay

Dee Smith &
Jeanne Goldhaber

Redleaf Press
St. Paul, Minnesota
www.redleafpress.org

Published by Redleaf Press
a division of Resources for Child Caring
10 Yorkton Court
St. Paul, MN 55117
Visit us online at www.redleafpress.org

© 2004 Dee Smith and Jeanne Goldhaber
Cover designed by Cathy Spengler
Interior typeset in Veljovic Book and Zemke Hand
and designed by Cathy Spengler

Redleaf Press books are available at a special discount when purchased
in bulk (1,000 or more copies) for special premiums and sales promo-
tions. For details, contact the sales manager at 800-423-8309.

Library of Congress Cataloging-in-Publication Data

Smith, Dee, 1949-
    Poking, pinching, and pretending : documenting toddlers'
explorations with clay / Dee Smith and Jeanne Goldhaber.
       p. cm.
    ISBN 1-929610-48-3
    1. Play. 2. Toddlers. 3. Modeling. 4. Early childhood education.
5. Participant observation. I. Title: Documenting toddlers'
explorations with clay. II. Goldhaber, Jeanne. III. Title.
HQ782.S62 2004
649'.51—dc22

          2003028138

Manufactured in the United States of America
11 10 09 08 07 06 05 04   1 2 3 4 5 6 7 8

Contents

Foreword

*We must observe their faces, their eyes, and their hands, because
it is here that words, actions, and feelings are born. It is here that
we find the meaning of what they do. . . . We may have the chance
to understand better how action, communication, and social interaction are indisputable sources of thought refinement, cognitive
development, cooperative learning and also the source of the power-
ful tool that is language, even before it becomes verbal. The more
we are convinced of this, the more our educational theories and our
attitudes toward the world of young children will express higher
expectations and greater respect.*

••• Loris Malaguzzi, *The Little Ones of Silent Movies: Make-Believe with Children and Fish
at the Infant-Toddler Center*

I have fresh in my mind the pleasure and satisfaction I felt
each time Dee Smith brought me up to date with photographs
and stories about the explorations and discoveries of clay by
Andrew, Eric, Collin, Maria, Natalie, Ethan, and Joey, along
with their teacher, Kimberly. It has been a privilege to follow
the shared reflections and serious determination of the com-
mitted group of educators at the University of Vermont Campus
Children's Center. From the time they initiated their investigations of how young children become literate, focusing on beginning communications that include gesture, language, and
media, I have been an interested follower of their research,
particularly the questions they were framing.

How do children communicate before language or at the
beginning of their language development? How do adults read
their nonverbal language? How do we give meaning to their
intentions in order to support their journey into discovery and
rediscovery? How do we interpret what we observe? How do
we help children to know and learn with confidence? Such are
the kinds of questions they have been developing.

When we prepare for our daily encounters with young children in a context of attentive care, and when we offer materials
that can be transformed, we create avenues to participate in the

experience without invasion. We can give ourselves the ease of observing children with attention and questions, to start to discover the range of their repertoire of strategies, their emerging skills, and their abilities to make connections and inventions. As we give credit to the children for their unique potentials we should also be aware of our own interests and subjectivity as we work with them. By sharing points of view about the complexity and beauty of what we observe, together we can construct interpretations that open for us new meanings of children's thoughts and actions.

These authors have accompanied the children in their adventure with clay. They have observed attentively the direction of their gaze, the language of their hands and bodies, and have seen how the children—each one in a personal way—have been able to capture the essence of this material. The children have given an identity to the clay, constructing relationships and transformations and creating often unexpected forms. This process led the children to feel pleasure and competence and the teachers to have new perceptions and perspectives on the value of the children's interaction with clay.

Now Dee Smith and Jeanne Goldhaber have made the learning experience of this community visible to other educators. This engaging book opens up possibilities for teachers to see young children in close encounters with a flexible material, to notice adults creating a context that can transform those encounters into layers of discoveries, to read the teachers' informed reflections, and to realize how communication can bring to light children's ideas and theories. All through this narrative we sense this group of adults' deep-set beliefs in the potential of children and their accumulated expertise in the qualities and potential of this generous, rich material. Through their documentation we see the combination of these two beliefs: a belief in the potential of children and a belief in the power of the material. This combination has produced, as an outcome of this study, new interpretations of early development in the process of nurturing the *old* language of clay.

Lella Gandini
July 2003

Introduction

In this book a team of early childhood educators shares a story that reflects our context, pedagogy, and values. The experiences we describe in the following pages took place at the University of Vermont (UVM) Campus Children's Center. The UVM Campus Children's Center is an early education and care program that serves as both a lab school for the Early Childhood PreK–3 Teacher Education Program and as an early education and care center for the children of university faculty, staff, and students. The Campus Children's Center is a small program that serves a total of forty children, including infants, toddlers, and preschoolers. There are four classrooms, each staffed by two mentor teachers. The infant-toddler program and preschool are coordinated by head teachers who also teach university courses and supervise staff and student teachers. Faculty members of the Early Childhood Program are very involved in the life of the center, and correspondingly, center staff participates in the academic program as co-instructors, guest lecturers, and mentor teachers. Like all programs, however, the true identity of the Campus Children's Center is much more complex and nonlinear than its affiliation, address, and demographics suggest. Rather, its identity is a story of change and evolution, a story that explains at least in part how and why we decided to write this book.

The Campus Children's Center: A Story of Change

The Campus Children's Center began its life in the mid-1950s as the Early Childhood Development Center, a part-time lab school. It was housed in the ground floor of the Home Economics building on the main campus and then moved to a nearby but off-campus space. In the early 1970s it moved yet again to its current location, the Living Learning Complex, in what was then a programmatically and architecturally innovative complex of buildings that still includes student suites, academic offices, and university classrooms as well as the Center.

Not only the Center's name and physical location has changed over time, but also its mission. As a part-time lab school, it was designed to provide the undergraduate majors of the Early Childhood and Human Development program with a setting in which to learn about young children, families, and the practice of early childhood education. In the 1980s the Early Childhood faculty became particularly interested in the constructivist perspective, and looked to the writings of Piaget (1954), Kamii and DeVries (1978), Forman and Kuschner (1983), and Duckworth (1987) to integrate a constructivist perspective into both the academic program and the lab school. As a result, the academic program and the Center developed a pedagogy that relied heavily on observation and the use of video to develop experiences for the children based on their interests, questions, and past experiences.

In the early 1990s two changes converged to transform the center once again. One change involved the demographics of the university. With more women on the faculty, the University's Board of Trustees was faced with an increasing demand for on-site child care. After countless committee meetings, surveys, and reports, the Center experienced a rebirth to its current identity: an on-site, full-day, year-round program for children, ages six weeks to five years, of the University of Vermont's faculty, staff, and students. Its mission was now two-fold: to provide early education and care to the UVM campus community and to continue to serve as a lab school for the Early Childhood PreK–3 Teacher Education Program.

At about the same time, program faculty and center staff began to hear about the municipal infant-toddler programs and preschools in Reggio Emilia, Italy. Several of us participated in a study tour in 1991 and again in 1993, this time with a particular interest in studying how Italian educators used written observations, transcriptions, photographs, and videotapes to document the children's experiences in their program. We were inspired by Vea Vecchi's description of documentation as "an indispensable source of materials that we use everyday to be able to 'read' and reflect critically, both individually and collectively, on the experience we are living, the project we are exploring" (Vecchi 1993, 122). Could our use of observation and videotape in our program be enriched by what we had seen, heard, and read about in Reggio Emilia?

Upon our return, we decided to pursue this question in our center, while in the process of reinventing ourselves as a community of infants, toddlers, preschoolers, families, and teachers. At first, the teachers in each classroom worked independently to explore the use of photography, videotape, and written observation to strengthen their practice. Finally, in 1997, the infant room and preschool teachers decided to embark on a shared investigation of the preschoolers' interest in babies. We discussed their observations of the children's interactions and the preschoolers' theories about infants at our weekly center staff meetings. This experience contributed to our sense of being members of a shared enterprise: our study of the use of documentation to strengthen our practice was bringing us together as a learning community.

The following year, all the teachers decided to participate in an investigation of how young children become literate. Each week, one of the classrooms presented examples of the children's efforts to "make meaning" through gesture, oral and written language, and drawing. We read observations of infants communicating where they wanted to go for a walk by leaning in their teachers' arms in a particular direction; we watched videotapes of toddlers "reading" *The Three Billy Goats Gruff* and then reenacting it again and again and again; and we discussed preschoolers' messages to each other that reflected not only their emerging understanding of the relationship between oral and written language, but also their growing appreciation of the power of print as a means to communicate emotions, desires, and ideas.

This investigation not only contributed to our understanding of how young children become literate, but it also played a significant role in our study of the use of documentation as a cycle of inquiry (Gandini and Goldhaber 2001). We learned the value of developing a question or series of questions to help us clarify the topic of our investigation, which in turn helped us determine which observation strategies to use. We developed new systems, such as the use of loose-leaf notebooks to organize related observations, photographs, and artifacts in chronological order. This seemingly simple strategy allowed us easy access to the material we were collecting, which in turn supported our efforts to review, analyze, and extend the children's experiences.

But perhaps most important, our study of children's development as meaning-makers changed how we saw ourselves. Yes, we were teachers, caregivers, and mentors, but this experience expanded our role to one that could potentially affect the quality of not only our own practice and knowledge base but that of the larger professional community as well. In short, it taught us to see ourselves as teacher-researchers within a learning community.

Teacher-Researchers

The idea of teacher-researchers inspired Dee Smith, head teacher of the Infant-Toddler Program, to study young children's use of clay. She found a willing and vitally important collaborator in the young toddler room. Mentor teacher Kimberly Waterman was interested in how young children might engage with clay, and agreed to be the supporting teacher throughout the investigation. Both Dee and Kimberly believed that clay's transformative properties made it an ideal medium for even the youngest of children, as is strikingly evident in the incredibly detailed and expressive ceramic lions sculpted by preschoolers in *To Make a Portrait of the Lion*, a videotaped documentary from the Villetta School in Reggio Emilia, Italy. These images contributed to Dee and Kimberly's desire to look closely at children's very early experiences with this organic, highly malleable medium.

Dee began by framing her question broadly, asking how young children develop an understanding of the medium of clay. Over time, many more specific questions emerged as Dee and Kimberly observed the toddlers' interactions with clay. Each new set of questions prompted further experiences with clay and further discussion, which led to more questions in a continuous cycle of observation, analysis, and experience. Throughout this process, Dee and Kimberly discussed the videotapes of children's explorations as often as possible. Dee and Jeanne Goldhaber, a faculty member of the Early Childhood Program, met regularly to analyze observations and plan future encounters to support, challenge, and learn more about the children's interactions with clay. Occasionally we were fortunate enough to have Dee, Jeanne, Kimberly, and other teachers available to discuss the meaning of children's explorations. Ultimately Dee and Jeanne collaborated to write this book.

Overview

In this little book we share some of the many clay stories that have come out of these experiences. In chapters 1, 2, and 3, we share stories of our initial investigation of a group of toddlers' first encounters with clay. In chapters 4 and 5 we follow several of these children as they become increasingly knowledgeable about clay and more intentional in their use of it. Chapter 6 describes the work of another group of children that has been engaged with clay since infancy.

These chapters are organized to reflect the investigation cycle. We begin each discussion of the children's interactions with clay with questions that helped to clarify what we wanted to learn and to decide what and how we would observe. We include these questions—even some that remained unresolved— to draw you into our process and to invite you to construct your own theories about the meaning of the children's work as it develops. Related observations and images follow, which we then analyze in terms of their possible meaning. Finally, we share decisions we made about how to respond and reenter the cycle by framing the questions that helped us begin a new round of observation.

In the afterword, Barbara Burrington, the preschool program head teacher, reflects on the children's work, now that they are preschoolers using this medium they came to know and love as toddlers. Her thoughtful comments remind us that this book is not just about clay, but about an entire system of relationships that gives our program its unique identity as a community.

Taken together these chapters document our journey as teacher-researchers. We are humbled by our mistakes and uneasy at the prospect of making them public. Yet, we are also proud of our story and are grateful to the educators of

Reggio Emilia, who have inspired us to take responsibility for not only generating knowledge, but for sharing it with our colleagues as well. We are particularly grateful to Lella Gandini for her unwavering support as our program continues to reinvent itself in the face of our unique challenges and opportunities. Above all, this book reflects how privileged we are to be members of a community that so clearly values collaboration, inquiry, and engagement. The work reported here could never have been accomplished had it not been for the support we received at every step along the way. We are indebted to all the Campus Children's Center teachers, children and families, students and program faculty, but above all, we are most grateful to seven toddlers whose curiosity, wisdom, and stout hearts inspired our vision and nurtured our spirits. It is our pleasure to introduce the protagonists of our story. Here are the toddlers whose explorations with clay you will follow as you read the rest of the book:

Andrew (18 months)

Ethan (27 months)

Maria (19 months)

Natalie (27 months)

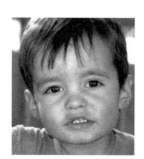

Joey (27 months)

Collin (22 months)

Erik (19 months)

References

Duckworth, Eleanor. 1987. *"The having of wonderful ideas"
and other essays on teaching and learning.* New York:
Teachers College Press.

Forman, George. 1999. Beyond the attentive eye: The
importance of theory for the practice of documentation.
Canadian Children 24: 4–8.

Forman, George, and David Kuschner. 1983. *The child's
construction of knowledge: Piaget for teaching children.*
Washington, DC: National Association for the Education
of Young Children.

Gandini, Lella, and Jeanne Goldhaber. 2001. Two reflections
on documentation: Documentation as a tool for promoting
the construction of respectful learning. In *Bambini: the
Italian approach to infant/toddler care,* eds. Lella Gandini
and Carolyn Edwards. New York: Teachers College Press.

Kamii, Constance, and Rheta DeVries. 1978. *Physical knowledge
in preschool education: Implications of Piaget's theory.*
Englewood Cliffs, NJ: Prentice-Hall.

Piaget, Jean. 1954. *The construction of reality in the child.*
New York: Basic Books.

Vecchi, Vea. 1993. The role of the Atelierista: An interview
with Lella Gandini. In *The hundred languages of children:
The Reggio Emilia approach to early childhood education,*
eds. Lella Gandini, Carolyn Edwards, and George Forman.
Norwood, NJ: Ablex.

Chapter 1
First Encounters with Clay

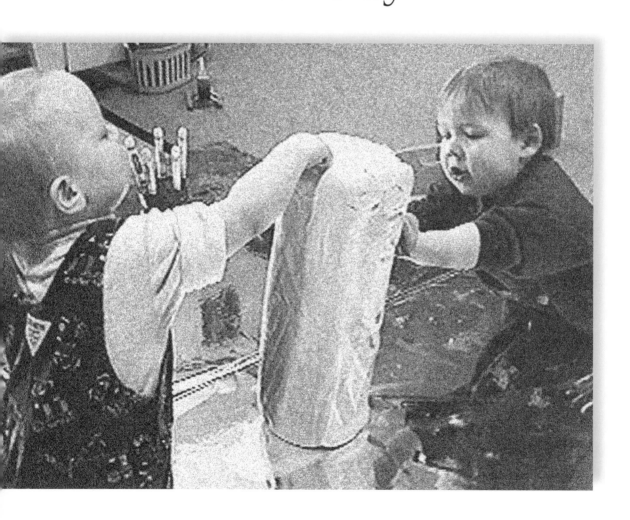

Beginning with Questions

How do toddlers explore clay? What questions do young
children have during their initial explorations of the clay?
What do the children understand about the medium of clay?

Before beginning this study, we had given the children few
opportunities to interact with clay, although we had offered
them many opportunities to use other media such as markers,
paint, blocks, and playdough. We predicted that because of
its novelty, the children would explore the clay in much the
same way they had interacted with these more familiar materials when they were first presented. Therefore, we expected
to observe the children exploring the clay's physical properties through actions such as mouthing, smelling, patting, and
banging, as well as by combining it with other objects in the
environment.

Initial Observations

During our first three sessions the clay was presented to all seven children as one large cylinder. We began with the large cylinder because, quite frankly, we did not know how else to begin and because we had observed in the past that toddlers often enjoy exploring large quantities of media. Because we had usually supported the children's playdough explorations by adding a variety of objects or tools, we also made available several poking tools during their first clay encounters. We covered the table tops with sheets of mylar because the color of the tables was similar to that of the clay. We wanted the children to be able to notice any traces the clay left on the surface. In retrospect, a dark-colored covering would have been more effective.

We made the following observations and images of the children as they initially encountered this large mass of clay.

A Large Clay Cylinder

Andrew and Erik poke the clay cylinder repeatedly. They scrape it with their fingers and then reattach the resulting small pieces they have scraped away. They explore the clay's stickiness as they try diligently to pick it from their fingers.

Several children explore the weight of the clay. Early on they try to push the clay over, but its sheer mass keeps it

upright. Eventually, however, multiple attempts at their goal produce the desired results. The children are startled when the tall cylinder topples loudly onto its side. "Uh oh!" they exclaim. Maria looks to her teacher and

says with surprise, "Heavy!" The children try to pick up the clay; they push at the mass without success. The clay stays in its now horizontal position.

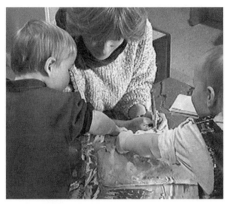

All the children are very interested in the physical properties of the clay. They poke, pat, scrape, mouth, lick, inspect, squeeze, pound, roll, push, smell, and pull at the clay.

Collin, who routinely runs cars and trucks over various surfaces of the classroom, brings a vehicle to the clay. His friends join him in rolling vehicles over the clay.

Collin also brings his favorite animal figures to the clay and pokes them into its soft surface. Other children show their excitement over this new relationship Collin is exploring between the novel and the familiar.

The children gather around the clay to inspect the holes. They joyfully share their discoveries with each other.

Reflecting on Our Observations

Our observations both confirmed our predictions about how children would explore the clay and uncovered patterns of exploration and interaction that we had not anticipated. As we expected, the children spent a great deal of time exploring the physical properties of the clay. They wanted to know how this new object felt, looked, tasted, and smelled. However, the very nature of clay invited different forms of exploration than did markers, paint, blocks, and playdough. For example, the children were intrigued by the clay's resistance to being moved or lifted. Its stickiness and malleability encouraged a wide range of exploratory actions that markers, paints, and blocks did not, such as poking, scraping, and squeezing. Taken together, the clay's heft, stickiness, and malleability challenged the children's prior knowledge and invited new combinations of exploration.

The children also incorporated prior interests and play schemes with familiar objects into their clay exploration. For example, in the very first session with clay, Collin rolled vehicles over the surface of the clay just as he had previously rolled them over the classroom's carpets, railings, and blocks.

The extent to which the children shared their discoveries with each other was an unexpected but welcome surprise. We thought the children would be more self-absorbed in the clay, but throughout these first encounters they looked to one another, sharing their joy and discoveries.

We were also particularly interested in—and curious about—the children's continuous attempts to fragment the large cylinder of clay. For the most part they were unsuccessful in their efforts, seeming to lack sufficient strength and dexterity to break the clay down into smaller units. We wondered if the children attempted to fragment the clay because they had a desire to work with smaller, more manageable pieces, or if they had another idea in mind.

Next Steps

Reflecting on our observations helped us to think more clearly about our next presentation of clay to the children. We decided to present the clay as small individual slabs, preformed clay balls, and fat coils. While we hoped these smaller forms would make the clay easier to fragment, we also wondered whether presenting the clay in smaller pieces would change how the children interacted not only with the clay, but also with each other. Would the smaller pieces prompt new types of investigations? Had the large single cylinder contributed to the sociability of the play? Would having smaller pieces interrupt the shared joy of the experience? While the children paid little attention to the tools we provided in these early sessions, we wondered what role they would play in the future. The following two chapters highlight the children's experiences when clay is presented in these smaller forms.

Chapter 2
Individual
Offerings of Clay

Beginning with Questions

During the next few sessions, clay was offered to all the children in thick slabs, approximately 9 inches in diameter. How would they respond to the thick, smooth surfaces? A few coils and balls, most of which had been made by busy adult hands as the sessions progressed, were also available. We wondered how these new presentations of clay would affect the children's explorations. Would the children be more self-absorbed and focused on their own clay pieces while exploring individual portions of clay?

Observations

The children focused immediately and intensely on the individual slabs. They patted the clay, poked deeply with tools and their fingers, lifted the slabs high into the air, and squealed with delight! There was a hum of satisfaction and exploration around the table. Eventually, children began to notice their peers' explorations. Sometimes they would thrust a ball of clay toward their peers, as if asking for a shared confirmation of meaning. The following observations and images capture the essence of many of the children's experiences:

Clay Slabs: Poking and Cars

Remember Collin? Initially he brought animals and vehicles to his exploration of clay. Collin returns, bringing a car to the table and running it over the smooth flat surface of a slab of clay. As he runs the car over the clay,

Collin explores further by poking his finger multiple times into its soft surface. He checks the wheels of the car. Then he lifts the clay slab and looks underneath.

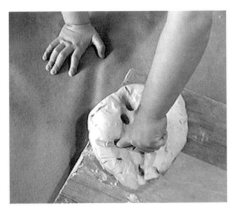

Maria pokes deeply into the clay. After repeated pokes, she lifts the clay and checks the surface on the other side. Seeing the smooth surface, she turns the clay over and begins to investigate its properties anew.

Natalie pokes a slab of clay with several small tools. She presses a small ball of clay on top of her slab, and then pokes at her new structure with one of the tools.

Later, Natalie hunches over the clay slab with a small tool in hand. Her face is close to the clay as she holds the tool like a pen, making marks in the clay.

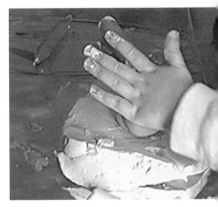

During the second presentation of smaller pieces of clay, Kimberly molds a slab into a long tube. Collin and Erik watch as the form takes shape. "Choo-choo train!" exclaims Collin. He points repeatedly to the edge of the clay tube. Erik observes Collin's actions, and says, "Tunnel," as he points to the end of the clay tube. Both boys continue their dialogue of "choo-choo" and "tunnel," repeating their words, as if to clarify the meaning.

Reflecting on the Observations These observations advanced our thinking about children's exploration with clay. By offering small slabs we temporarily lost some of the sociability of the investigation as the children approached the clay with their individual questions. They turned to share their discoveries with each other only after a period of individual inquiry. All the children showed intense interest in these small, individual clay slabs; those who had spent only a few minutes at a time with the large cylinder now spent lengthy periods of time engaged with the material.

Poking to Learn about Clay The children explored the physical properties of the clay in many ways. They scraped, tasted, smelled, pounded, and pinched it. However, poking was the most frequent form of exploration. We had several theories about the children's desire to poke. Perhaps the children poked repeatedly because the outcome of their actions contradicted knowledge they had constructed about the impenetrability of objects. Other materials they used, such as unit and hollow blocks, were resistant to poking, while pressing down on a block provided a different sensory experience and feedback. A block remains solid, whereas clay gives way to the pressure of children's fingers. Perhaps clay's responsiveness to the child's actions encouraged this aggressive and repetitive form of inquiry.

After watching the tapes several times, we also realized that when poked, the clay became a mold that enveloped the children's fingers and that, depending on its force and angle, each poke offered new results. Perhaps Maria's investigation with deep pokes offered her a playful exploration with this functional relationship (Forman and Kuschner 1983). Did she repeat the action over and over to confirm this change, or to assess the varying results? When she pushed her finger farther into the clay, the hole became deeper, and her finger less visible—a kind of dialogue she repeated over and over. Or perhaps this was a playful test of object permanence, a toddler version of "peek-a-boo," as she made her finger disappear and reappear?

Examining the Slabs' Underside Repeatedly we saw children pick up their slabs to look underneath. They never picked up the slab immediately, but only after they made a number of marks on the surface of the clay. Sometimes the children continued their exploration on top of the clay. More frequently, however, the children turned the slab over and made marks on the underside. We had many questions about the meaning of these actions. For example, in the photo on page 9 we wondered what Maria was thinking as she turned over the clay. Did she expect to see marks? Perhaps Maria was asking why the hole was not visible on the other side. When she turned the clay over and began to investigate its properties again, we wondered if she was trying to re-create the holes from her earlier exploration, or perhaps the smooth surface of the clay was so inviting that it demanded a new exploration.

Discovering the Complexity of Clay Young children constantly explore how materials relate to each other and these children readily included the clay in their relational play. They explored the relationship of clay to clay, their favorite toys to the clay, and the tools to clay. We saw this experimentation earlier in Natalie's exploration with tools on the clay slabs and in Collin's exploration of his truck on the clay. Returning to the vignette involving Collin's slab, we discussed the meaning of the relationship he was exploring between his car and the clay. He may have been exploring the depth of the tracks or perhaps he was verifying the movement of the car by running his fingers along the tracks. When he checked the underside of his car did he think there was a problem with the wheels, or was he developing a theory about the relationship between the tracks and the wheels?

While we continued to observe relational play throughout the toddler classroom, we realized that the responsive nature of clay added opportunities for experimentation and yielded surprise as the material was transformed, providing more complex possibilities for challenging children's thinking. For example, as Natalie pushed the small tool into the clay over and over again, she may have been validating her new knowledge of this material while exploring the relationship between the force of her push and the depth of the resulting marks. As she stacked a clay ball on top of her slab, she pushed hard to press the clay together with the force of her body. We had not observed this technique when Natalie or the other children stacked blocks.

Natalie's use of tools is also interesting. She repeatedly used tools to make small marks in the clay. Her body posture and pencil grip are reminiscent of children's early efforts to write with pencil and paper. Because we had seen Natalie (as well as several other toddlers) begin to use markers and paint to represent or depict real events and objects, we believed it was quite possible that she was exploring clay as yet another surface on which to write or draw.

Children Share Meaning In the observation of Collin and Erik, we watched the children use their emerging vocabulary to share an understanding of the meaning of the clay tube. Their verbal exchange suggested to us that they understood that clay could represent recalled objects or experiences. Perhaps the clay tube recalled a well-loved book in the classroom about a train that traveled through tunnels. In *Young Children's Sculpture and Drawing,* Claire Golomb (1974) refers to this level of representational thinking as "reading" off the material.

Revisiting Our Questions

We began these sessions asking whether the way we presented the clay would affect the children's exploration. It was clear that presenting the clay in individual pieces rather than as a single large cylinder provoked less social play, at least in the beginning. However, we hypothesized that this might be a necessary step while the children became more familiar with the medium and the types of exploration the clay would support. The small pieces of clay confirmed for us the importance of poking, which we had seen with the large cylinder of clay. It was again a primary mode of exploration. While we can't say definitively why the children spent so much of their time poking the clay, we theorized that the children may have been exploring the responsiveness of this very malleable medium, perhaps investigating the functional relationship between the act of poking and the depth and angle of the resulting hole. We even considered the possibility that the children were testing or perhaps confirming their understanding of the permanence of the physical world of objects by playing with the appearance and disappearance of their fingers as they poked the clay again and again.

The slabs of clay, however, brought new and unanticipated forms of exploration. We were curious about why, after marking on the surface of clay slabs, the children repeatedly checked the underside of their slabs, often turning them over to begin anew. We thought about Collin, in particular, who repeatedly checked under the clay after rolling his car over the surface. Did he think the tracks would be visible underneath, or were the imprints from the car so light that he thought the marks might be hidden under the clay? Was he satisfied when he found there were no marks? In turning the slab over, was it possible that Collin was asking questions about the clay's identity: "Is this the same object now that I've made these marks?" We thought it possible that the children's expectations were so violated that they needed to confirm their answers many, many times. The children's growing understanding of the responsiveness of the material may also have invited them to repeat their actions when the clean surface reappeared.

We began to question *when* children begin to represent what they know and experience. Collin and Eric's shared reference to the clay as a tunnel and the intensity of Natalie's effort to make marks on the clay seemed to support a level of representation that we do not typically expect in children this young. Simultaneously, we thought about a humorous moment when Maria put a ball of clay on her head, perhaps in an act of balance, but just as possibly as a pretend hat. We asked ourselves whether young children use clay as a medium to represent objects and ideas earlier than we thought. We wondered if relying on language to verify children's representational intent might be inadequate when children are only beginning to acquire the skills necessary to use a new medium. In other words, it seemed possible that the product of the children's efforts might not reflect the meaning of their actions. We were learning yet again the importance of "listening closely" (Rinaldi 2001) not only to the children's words and gestures, but also to their sometimes seemingly awkward but potentially meaningful manipulation of this new medium.

Next Steps

The children's investigations were rich and varied. We were beginning to formulate theories about the meaning of their interactions with the clay, but we had many questions—we still had so much to learn from watching the children! The children were very engaged during the clay sessions, making discoveries, formulating their own theories, investigating their questions. With this in mind, we agreed to give both the children and ourselves the gift of time and to continue to present the clay as slabs, coils, and balls. We looked forward to watching the children as they became more experienced with this incredibly versatile medium.

References

Forman, George, and David Kuschner. 1983. *The child's construction of knowledge: Piaget for teaching children.* Washington, DC: National Association for the Education of Young Children.

Golomb, Claire. 1974. *Young children's sculpture and drawing: A study in representational development.* Cambridge: Harvard University Press.

Rinaldi, Carla. 2001. The pedagogy of listening: The listening perspective from Reggio Emilia. *Innovations* 8: 1–4.

Chapter 3

Toddlers As Mathematicians

Beginning with Questions

For the past three sessions the children had been offered clay in slabs, coils, and balls. We observed that the children were very interested in this format and both they and the teachers seemed to have ample questions and hypotheses. We decided to continue presenting the clay in smaller pieces to the whole group, and we wondered if this presentation would continue to engage their exploration with the medium. Would our observations with this format continue to offer us new insight into the children's inquiry? Would the children signal that it was time for a change?

The observations from this session are rich and varied. Rather than analyzing them collectively, we will discuss each observation individually.

Exploring Mass, Velocity, Sound, Stability

It is a cold, spring morning and the heat is turned up in the classroom. With their teachers' help, many toddlers have removed their clothing down to just diapers. All seven children are present and are looking forward to working with clay. Dee has prepared large chunks of clay in slabs, balls, and coils. A few pieces of clay are left in undefined but interesting forms.

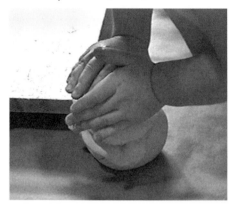

Natalie carefully stacks balls of clay. She leans forward, pressing on the clay with all her weight. On many occasions the children seem to categorize the shape of balls by placing one on top of another. Several of the children show us their understanding that you must press down in order for the balls to remain stacked.

The children notice the heaviness of the clay. Many of the children pick up the clay, straining from its weight. Others exclaim, "Heavy!" or "Big, so big!"

. . .

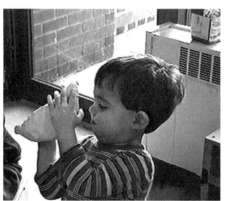

We observed children picking up large pieces of clay and dropping them on the table again and again. We hypothesized that they might have found several aspects of this action interesting. They might have been exploring the weight of the clay, the sound of the clay as it hit the table, or possibly the reaction of the clay (which did not roll but rather abruptly stopped moving as soon as it landed on the table). Perhaps the clay violated the children's expectations. As we had seen so often, young children actively test out their theories many times before accommodating their old theories to knowledge gained from new experiences.

• • •

Ethan places two long coils of clay side-by-side and runs his hands over the surface. Ethan may be categorizing the shapes or comparing the lengths of the coils as he runs his hands over the surface, acknowledging the relationship between the two coils.

Ethan begins the process of fragmenting a coil into smaller parts, using a tool to "cut" the clay into many pieces. This procedure is similar to actions we have seen many times. Usually, however, the children scrape or pull off the tiniest bits possible, creating miniature segments of clay.

Andrew examines a large ball of clay that is partially sliced down the middle and opens like a book. He seems intrigued by this particular configuration of clay and repeatedly opens and closes the two sides. He places a large coil of clay where the two pieces meet, and then tries to bring the halves together. The size of the coil prevents the halves meeting, but he continues to repeat his actions, investigating this relationship between the halves and the coil.

• • •

Andrew's initial exploration might have reflected an interest in the parts that make up this whole, but the investigation became more interesting when he introduced the coil. What was he thinking about? Was this a game of object permanence? Perhaps he wanted to play "hide and seek" with the coil. Or did he have ideas about the malleability of the clay? Andrew had experimented before with pushing small pieces of clay into a larger slab. Did he think he could press the large coil into the hinged piece of clay? Did Andrew have a vision of how these pieces of clay might be transformed? We had so many theories!

• • •

Erik notices several small holes in the clay. He takes a thin coil, which Kimberly has formed, and tries to put it in some of the holes.

• • •

Erik was demonstrating his ability to gauge the size of the clay to the size of the hole, a skill that children appear to master early in life. Through trial and error, Erik learned important information about the clay's properties. The clay coil bent so that he was unable to insert it into the hole. This experience contrasted with the metal and plastic tools he used, and even with his own fingers. These objects easily penetrated the clay's soft surface and simultaneously maintained their own shape and substance. Perhaps Erik remembered this information in a later session when he returned to his exploration of objects in holes. That time he took multiple pokers and inserted them into a piece of clay. He then removed the blunt sticks, and checked the holes. Carefully he reinserted the sticks in an act of one-to-one correspondence.

• • •

Erik repeatedly giggles as he cradles a lump of clay balanced on the flat side of a pizza cutter. This new relationship of clay to tool takes on an element of humor, a kind of private toddler joke. He keeps this to himself, unaware of the camera or others around him. Perhaps he is amused by the weight of the clay, which is balanced on the tool, or perhaps he is assigning meaning to the clay. We will not know, since the form of the clay does not give our adult eyes a clue as to its meaning. Erik has been very interested in balls: perhaps he understands how difficult it is to balance a ball on another object.

Joey begins by placing a clay ball on top of a large wedge of clay. He releases his grip and the clay falls to the table. He tries several times, occasionally rocking the clay back and forth, or changing the position of the ball,

but each time he lets go, the clay ball falls. Across the table a friend has stacked three balls of clay.

Joey glances up, viewing the three stacked clay balls across the table. He takes his ball to this tower of clay and places it on top. The ball rolls to the table. After a few tries he returns to his own wedge of clay and tries once again to balance the ball on top.

• • •

The intensity of Joey's research and his attempt to substitute his peer's base for his own was interest-ing in itself. He was exchanging his base for one he had seen stacked with three balls. This sequence, however, raised other questions for us. Joey had been absent on several of the occa-sions when clay was first offered. We had seldom, if ever, seen him poke at the clay. Joey had also spent many hours playing with blocks, a material vastly different than clay and unrespon-sive to poking. We began to think again about the essential information that poking clay might offer the children. We theo-rized that this drive to poke, which so many of the children dis-played, gave them information necessary to form other rela-tionships with the clay. Perhaps poking offered the children knowledge about clay that informed their stack-ing with this medium. Or perhaps the children were learning about the responsiveness of the clay, or about its sticky quality? The signifi-cance we delegated to the act of poking increased.

• • •

Erik shows his surprise and joy after working to pierce the clay, forming a novel object.

A few days later we again find Erik with a piece of clay on the end of a clay tool. He carefully places the unsteady object on various surfaces and then releases his grip, testing the balance of his newly made object on multiple surfaces.

Andrew spears the clay with a dowel, appearing excited by the results. He discards the dowel and begins to spear the clay with a clay tool that has a loop of wire on the end. He struggles, treating this tool in the same way he did the dowel. He is unable, however, to pick up the clay. Using his other hand, he readjusts the clay several times. Finally his persistence pays off and he lifts the clay from the table.

. . .

In the three previous vignettes, Erik and Andrew used strategies of trial and error to accommodate old schemas or understandings to the task of combining tools with clay and using them to balance pieces of clay. We were convinced that this was a significant challenge to the children as they continued to explore variations of this relationship in future investigations.

Reflecting on Our Observations This session was so exciting! The children's interest in clay seemed to be building along with our own questions about their explorations. A problem, however, was beginning to surface as we looked over all our data. We had so many observations; we needed a way to organize and interpret our growing understanding of the children's inquiries. Dee and Jeanne stood in the hallway for an "on the fly" but significant conversation about the children's actions with clay and the organizational challenges we were facing. A variation on one of our original questions began to surface during the discussion. "What kinds of knowledge were the children building through their interactions with the clay?" Almost immediately the conversation turned to our constructivist roots, as we considered Piaget's discussions of children's exploration of the properties of the physical world and development of logical-mathematical and representational thinking.

Dee agreed to return to the tapes and to divide the observations of the children's interactions with the clay into these three categories. We were stunned by the results! Many of the children's interactions with the clay appeared to involve mathematical thinking. These observations seemed to mirror the research that Sinclair and colleagues discuss in *Infants and Objects,* which contains observations from child care centers in Paris. In these studies the researchers described the actions of very young children as precursors to logical, symbolic thinking (Sinclair et al. 1989). Indeed, looking over the latest clay session, we saw actions involving the exploration of weight, size, balance, fragmenting, comparing, and categorizing, as well as piercing the clay with a tool to form a new relationship. These explorations can be thought of as precursors to mathematical thinking. For example, Ethan's careful assessment of the two long coils, and his later action of fragmenting the coils into small pieces may contribute to his understanding of measurement in the future.

Other examples involved the construction of new relationships between two objects. We saw both Erik and Andrew involved in inquiries that connected a small piece of clay to a tool. Erik and Andrew had to have already understood many properties of the two objects (clay and tool) in order to construct their new object. In *Number in Preschool and Kindergarten,* Kamii (1982) refers to Piaget's description of this act as reflective abstraction, meaning a construction by the mind rather than a focus on isolated properties of an object. This reflects Piaget's view of logico-mathematical thinking in that both children assessed the properties (and possibilities) of the clay and a tool, and had formed an expectation that the tool could pierce the clay to create a new object.

New Questions Emerge

Our thinking and discussions after this clay session gave new life to our study. Recognizing the children's actions as evidence of prelogical thought, we also realized how much we had been focusing on children individually. While our strategy was giving us information about the specific children we were taping, we questioned what we were missing. Moreover, our reading about small group learning in *Municipal Infant-Toddler and Preschool Centers in Reggio Emilia* (Malaguzzi 1998, 94) challenged us to consider turning our attention to how small groups of two or three children would to co-construct meaning with clay as the shared medium.

References

Forman, George. 1999. Beyond the attentive eye: The importance of theory for the practice of documentation. *Canadian Children* 24: 4.

Kamii, Constance. 1982. *Number in preschool and kindergarten.* Washington, DC: National Association for the Education of Young Children.

Malaguzzi, Loris. 1998. History, ideas, and basic philosophy: An interview with Lella Gandini. In *The hundred languages of children: The Reggio Emilia approach to early childhood education,* eds. Lella Gandini, Carolyn Edwards, and George Forman. Greenwich, CT: Ablex.

Sinclair, Hermine, Mira Stambeck, Irène Lézine, Sylvie Rayna, and MinaVerba. 1984. *Infants and objects: The creativity of cognitive development.* New York: Academic Press.

Chapter 4
Offering Clay in Small Groups

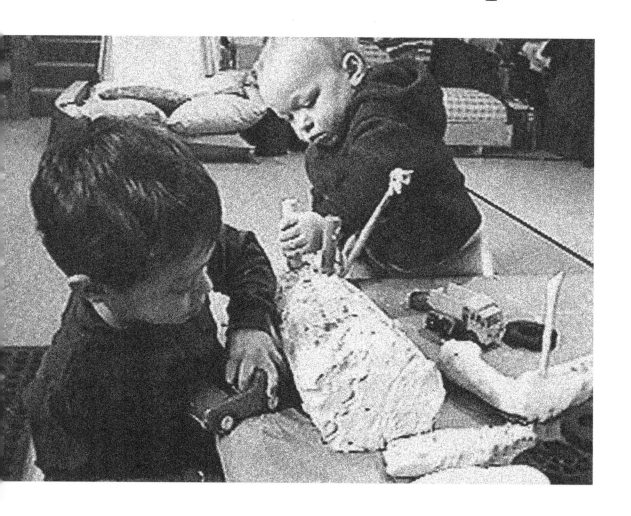

Beginning with Questions

We could see that children were becoming more familiar with clay and finding their own ways of experimenting with the medium. One of the challenges, however, was focusing on individual children while trying to support and engage the whole group. We asked ourselves two questions: How might our understanding change if we observed each child more closely? How might the children's investigation change if we were to offer clay in small groups? We reflected on the small group encounters we had been studying and reading about in the early childhood programs of Reggio Emilia and decided to divide the children into smaller groups. We hoped this strategy would not only allow us to study each child's use of clay more deeply, but allow the children to support each other's thinking in ways that might not have been possible in a larger group. Of course, as soon as we made this decision, we were faced with many other questions: Who should work together? What criteria would we use to form the groups? Should our decisions be based on the friendships we observed, or should they be based on the children's ways of investigating the clay? We had not deliberately paired children of this age before, so we had little experience to draw on. We worried that our decisions would be contrived and perhaps a bit artificial. We also had space constraints. Our classrooms are very small, and at that time we had no studio space for small groups of children. In the end, our decisions were based mostly on how the children investigated the medium, though we readily admit that at times the groupings depended on the flow of the day, the children who were present, and choices made by the toddlers. In this chapter we focus on several vignettes involving interactions between different pairs of children.

Small Group Observations

We began our small group investigation with Collin and Erik, two toddlers who often played together. We decided the remainder of the toddlers would explore the greater campus area with their other teacher, Catherine. Collin and Erik remained in the room and were offered the rare luxury of an extended period of Kimberly's time and each other's undivided attention. We were anxious to see how this setting might affect their exploration—whether they would be more focused, how they would explore the clay, and how they would interact with each other. This structure also gave us the opportunity to consider in depth the children's thinking and the potential that clay offered to their individual and collaborative explorations.

Erik and Collin Return to Familiar Props and Scripts

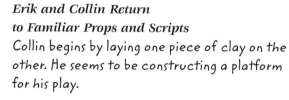

Collin begins by laying one piece of clay on the other. He seems to be constructing a platform for his play.

"I go get car!" says Collin. Collin returns with a car and uses the clay as a base for his vehicle play. He runs the car back and forth over his "road."

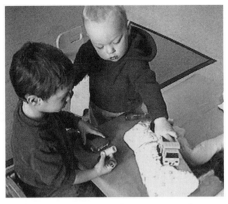

Erik pokes at a smaller piece of clay and exclaims, "Poke!" as he inserts his finger deep into the clay. As he pokes, he seems to be aware of Collin's actions with the vehicles on the clay. Eric leaves momentarily and returns with a dump truck to join Collin in running the vehicle over the clay's surface.

Erik abandons his play with the dump truck and returns to poking the clay, this time with a variety of tools. As he releases his hand from the tool, he checks the balance. When the tools don't stand upright, he pushes with more force. Sometimes Erik resets the tool into another spot.

Kimberly notices Erik's actions and begins parallel play. She starts by inserting a few tools into a smaller cylinder of clay. Erik observes Kimberly's work and adds tools to her lineup.

He is delighted with the result. "All ready!" he exclaims as he claps his hands together. "All ready truck!"

Erik begins to take the tools out of their holes. He lifts a tool, looks at the hole, and then resets it in the same place. Erik repeats his actions, either questioning the outcome or confirming his thinking.

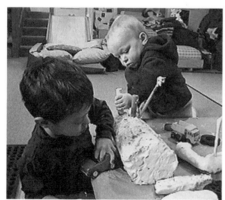

Erik brings a fat dowel over to the large cylinder of clay he was originally working on. He works to reset it again and is momentarily successful, but Collin removes it, laying it on the table. Erik tries once again to place the dowel in the hole, and this time it falls over.

He hands the tool to Kimberly and points to where the hole is. Kimberly says, "Right there? Can you help me?" When the tool doesn't remain in the hole a second time, Erik loses interest.

Reflecting on the Observation This was our first small group dialogue, and we found the children immediately returned to a familiar script and established a brief common focus. Erik began by trying to enter into Collin's play involving the truck and the clay. However, his deeper interest seemed to lie in the relationship between the tools and the clay. We had seen this relationship being explored on at least three occasions before: in chapter 2, Erik cradled the clay, which had been placed on top of the tool; in chapter 3, he speared the clay to form a new object; and again in chapter 3, he investigated, using trial-and-error, how speared clay balanced on various surfaces. It seemed to us that Erik was using his knowledge about the relationship between the tool's shape and the clay, and how the weight of clay on top of the tool affected the tool's ability to remain upright. In the above investigation Erik seemed to return to the concept of balance when he said, "All ready truck!" We hypothesized that Erik might be signaling his satisfaction that all the tools were inserted in the clay and remained upright.

Erik and the Clay Tool

Erik has a large ball of clay on the end of a wire tool. A hand is cupped below the ball, ready to capture any unintended fall. He gently holds his delicate construction as if protecting it from harm.

Reflecting on the Observation Although this observation was very brief, it was significant to us in that it captured a moment strikingly similar to the giggling vignette in chapter 3 when Erik cradled the clay that rested on the pizza cutter. In that moment Eric seemed to be demonstrating once again his knowledge of the clay's relationship to other objects. He seemed to understand that the tool could combine with the clay to form a new object, but that this combination was a bit fragile; that clay could separate from the wire cutter. This exploration of weight and balance was evident on many occasions as he worked with clay.

Collin and Erik: Choo-Choo

Collin pokes a tool into a clay ball.

 Collin: "Choo-choo train!"

 Kimberly: "Something about that looks like a choo-choo train?"

Collin makes another hole in the large tube and points to the hole.

 Collin: "A choo-choo train."

 Kimberly: "Is there a choo-choo train in here?" She points to the hole.

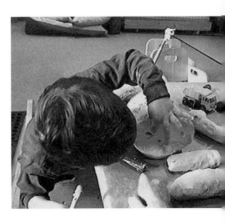

Collin: "Yeah!"

Kimberly: "Where?"

Collin: "In here!"

Kimberly picks up a large peg and pushes it into the side of the clay.

Kimberly: "If I make the hole bigger is it still a choo-choo train?"

Collin grabs the peg, "My turn." He pokes the holes continuously without words.

Erik picks up the dump truck and begins to drive it over the clay's surface saying, "Choo-choo, choo-choo."

Kimberly notices Erik's actions of running the truck over the clay. She thinks Collin may be interested in joining this game so she supports Erik's actions with her words.

Kimberly: "Choo-choo. Erik's driving that along and saying, 'Choo-choo, choo-choo.'"

Collin does not join Erik's play.

Reflecting on the Observation Almost a month had passed since Collin and Erik's first dialogue about the shape of the clay. At that time they appeared to share a common script about tunnels and trains. This time, however, their exploration involved common words, but possibly not a common meaning. Collin seemed to focus on the hole, accompanied by the words, "Choo-choo." He does not respond to Erik's actions of running the vehicle over the clay. For Collin, "Choo-choo" may be related to his previous reference to a train running through the tunnel. Erik's more literal action does not appear to connect with Collin's intentions.

Because of the length of the following vignette and the number of questions it generated, we will share some analysis with it as it unfolds.

Collin and the Dump Truck

As Erik runs the truck over the clay, Collin moves to Kimberly's lap, bringing his red car with him and placing it on the table. Kimberly attempts to reconnect Collin with the clay. She rolls a ball of clay and places it in the back of the car. "Remember when you went to get things to use with the clay and you chose the car?" She points to the car. Collin is immediately interested in this play.

He tries placing the large slab of clay in the back of the car.

Kimberly: "You're going to put that in the car. Do you think the car can carry that?" He pushes hard, but the clay doesn't fit.

Collin readjusts his thinking about what will fit in the back of the car. He begins to scrape small bits of clay from a slab, placing them in the car. Each time Collin presses hard on the clay pieces, molding them into one larger form in the back of the car.

• • •

Did Collin press hard on the clay so that more "pieces" would fit in the car? Or was he just "playing" with the properties of the clay? His goal might have been for the car to hold as much clay as possible, or perhaps he wanted to create a slab that fits into the back of the truck.

• • •

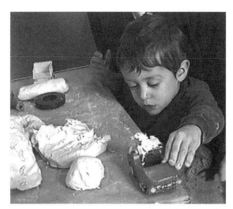

Kimberly: "Are you going to put more in the car? How do you get it to stick together so well?"

Collin does not answer but continues his task of filling the car with clay. In between filling the car with clay, Collin runs his vehicle back and forth across the table. He does this slowly and deliberately, watching the car move.

• • •

What was Collin focusing on as he watched the car move? Was it the movement of the wheel, the load of clay and possible attention to balance, or maybe his ability to control the speed? Though his questions remained unclear to us, certainly his intentions did not. Collin changed the variables and then observed the outcomes. This was an act of inquiry.

• • •

When Erik is finished with the dump truck, Collin begins to incorporate it into his play. He begins by taking all the clay out of the back of the car and loading it into the dump truck. Collin spends several minutes loading the dump

truck. When he has transferred all the clay from the car, he begins to pick at the small slab of clay, adding more clay to the truck. It seems that he wants the truck to be as full as possible. He runs the dump truck back and forth across the table as he did with the car. This time he runs it over the edge, but doesn't let go. He is carefully watching the truck as he does this.

Kimberly: "Where's the dump truck going to go with all that in it?"

Collin remains silent, but carefully manipulates the back of the truck to "dump" its load. The clay sticks to the truck and

does not come out. Collin repeats his action of trying to dump the contents several times.

Kimberly continues to narrate Collin's play. As Collin runs the truck over the clay's surface Kimberly states, "It's kind of bumpy. How'd it get so bumpy?" Collin seems very interested in the bumpiness of the clay. Kimberly supports this by creating a long, bumpy road for Collin's vehicle.

Collin rolls the truck along the clay road to the edge of the table, and this time he gently lowers it to the floor. Once again he explores the mechanics of "dumping" as he raises and lowers the back section. When the clay does not fall out of the truck he takes it out with his hand, and then puts it back in.

• • •

Collin brought a great deal of knowledge about inclines, as well as the properties of clay, to this encounter. His actions were very intentional, as he questioned why the clay didn't fall out of the truck bed. He repeatedly investigated the unexpected reaction of the clay to the tilt of the truck bed. When the clay didn't fall out, Collin seemed to reassure himself that the clay could in fact be taken out of the truck bed by removing it by hand.

• • •

Collin again rolls the dump truck over the long bumpy road. "Daddy's truck!" says Collin. He appears very excited.

Kimberly: "Does daddy drive a truck like that?"

Collin stops rolling the truck. He turns and waves his arms up and down while shaking his head, and smiling broadly. "Yeah!" Collin says, "Like this."

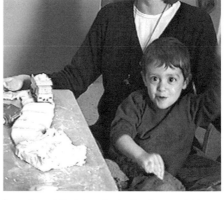

Collin seems to find all of this very funny. He laughs with his whole body, and then repeats the sequence of waving his arms and laughing several times.

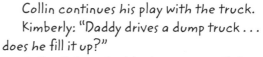

Collin continues his play with the truck.

Kimberly: "Daddy drives a dump truck . . . does he fill it up?"

Collin: "Yeah. Daddy driving truck." He again waves his arms up and down.

Kimberly: "What does he have loaded in his truck?"

Collin: "Dump truck."

Kimberly: "Who filled it up?"

We cannot understand Collin's answer. It sounds a little like "Dad did," but we remain uncertain.

Collin: "Daddy drive the truck!"

Kimberly: "Daddy drives it. Does he drive on bumpy roads like this?"

Collin: "Yeah!" He points to the window saying, "Window."

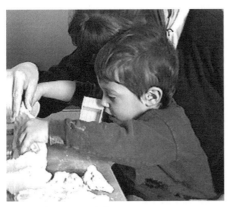

Kimberly: "There's a window on that truck."

Collin picks up the long bumpy road, and looks underneath. He seems interested in the smooth surface and turns the road over. He examines his "new" road.

Collin rolls the truck back and forth over the smooth clay surface. He seems to be exploring the contrast in the surfaces.

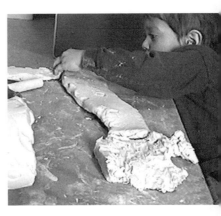

Reflecting on the Observation Collin's story intrigued us as we looked back over his play with the clay and vehicles. This story seemed as much about Collin and what it means to be a toddler as it was about his exploration of clay. For

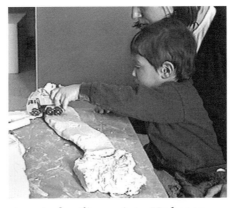

example, we saw Collin return to familiar scripts. He began by bringing his red car to the clay, a combination we had witnessed on many occasions. Collin was almost certainly exploring the clay's properties of weight, stickiness, and transformability. He also seemed to be recalling experiences he has had with his father. They were clearly pleasurable, even though we are quite possibly missing their full meaning. Collin embellishes the bumpiness of the road by waving his arms wildly and laughing wholeheartedly. Perhaps this is a kind of joke or game he plays with his father in their truck? Maybe Dad's arms go up and down as he exaggerates the bumps in the road? It is interesting to note that during this vignette Collin's parents were away on vacation and his grandparents were staying with him. It was certainly possible that Collin's separation from his parents explained his initial hesitation to engage with the clay and with Erik at the beginning of this experience. Collin seemed much more engaged when he moved to Kimberly's lap. From that secure position, he engaged with clay and vehicles for a long while, bringing recollections of his father into his script. We believed Collin was telling us a story rich in emotion, humor, and action—a story that he could not yet express with his verbal skills, but that the medium of clay could support.

Finally, at the end of this story we once again saw a familiar action as Collin lifted the clay to inspect the underside. The smooth surface, however, did not capture his attention for long. Perhaps it did not belong in the script of "bumpiness" that Collin had found so humorous.

On another morning we observed Natalie and Ethan, the two oldest children in the classroom at two-and-a-half. They were often found playing together, supporting each other through body language and words.

Ethan and Natalie: Popcorn

We offer Ethan and Natalie pieces of clay: slabs, large balls, and chunky cylinders. There are several tools around the table, including a rolling pin. Kimberly is at the table with children while Dee is videotaping. Ethan picks at his slab of clay, and small pieces begin to form on top of his slab.

Ethan: "This popcorn."

Kimberly: "All these pieces are popcorn?"

Ethan: "Yeah."

He places small pieces back into the clay. Natalie is nearby, but not involved in Ethan's exploration.

Dee: "Ethan says his clay is popcorn."

Natalie: "Popcorn?"

Ethan looks to Kimberly.

Ethan: "More."

Kimberly: "More what?"

Ethan: "More . . . popcorn."

Kimberly: "How could you get more popcorn?"

Ethan looks around, and his eyes settle on a cylinder of clay. He scrapes a small piece off the end.

Kimberly: "You got some more."

Ethan works diligently at collecting and forming small bits of clay. Each time he has a small piece he pushes it into the slab of clay.

Ethan: "Pop, pop, pop. Popping out!"

Kimberly: "You're popping it now."

Ethan: "Yeah!"

Kimberly: "You're pressing it into that piece of clay."

As Ethan works with the clay, Kimberly is using a rolling pin on another slab of clay.

Ethan: "Is there mine?"

Kimberly: "Would you like a turn?"

Ethan: "Yeah."

Ethan takes the small tool and begins rolling it on top of his clay in all directions, transforming the surface from bumpy to smooth.

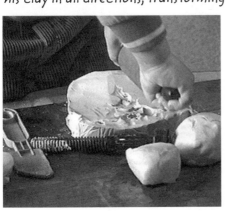

Kimberly: "What would you like to do with that rolling pin?"

Ethan: "Right here."

Kimberly: "What does it do to your big piece of clay?"

There is a pause, as Ethan remains silent.

Dee: "Ethan, where's your popcorn?"

Ethan: "It's in here." Ethan pats the clay with the end of the rolling pin.

Dee: "Is it hiding?"

Ethan: "Yeah! Can't find it!"

Dee: "I can't find it? Can you?"

Ethan: ". . . No."

Natalie: "I can find it for you, Ethan."

Natalie comes close to examine the clay.

Natalie: "Where is it?"

Ethan: "Right here." He points to the clay.

Natalie: "Is it under here?"

There is no response from Ethan, but he begins to pat the clay.

Kimberly: "How can we find it?"

Ethan continues to roll out the clay, resulting in the disappearance of all the popcorn. He tentatively puts his fingers into the clay again. He presses harder and begins to pull up some clay pieces.

Ethan: "I found some!"

Reflecting on the Observation While this interaction was fairly short in nature, it was notably different from our large group sessions in terms of the amount of uninterrupted time and teacher attentiveness. This opportunity allowed us a rare glimpse into a toddler's thinking that might have gone unnoticed, and most likely unsupported in a larger group setting.

Ethan encountered an unexpected yet classic problem of reversibility as he moved the rolling pin over the slab. Ethan's investigation of reversibility was supported both by Dee and

Kimberly's questions and by the transformational quality of the clay itself. In this vignette he confidently states his understanding that his popcorn is "here" in the clay, but then hesitates and seems a little confused when it is not visible. His friend Natalie came to his aid with her own idea of where they might find the missing popcorn. When Natalie became uncertain of why the popcorn was not visible, Ethan quietly continued to think through his dilemma.

It was unclear how intentional Ethan's actions were, but when he slowly began to dig into the clay again, small pieces reappeared. He rejoiced immediately at the appearance of the missing popcorn. His joy was evident as he exclaimed, "I found some!" What was not clear in this story is whether Ethan thought he found the same popcorn that "disappeared," or more popcorn.

Revisiting Our Observations

These five vignettes, as well as other small group encounters with clay, gave us an opportunity to revisit some of our thinking and questions. We were quite certain that observing children explore in small groups furthered our thinking about the children's investigations. The children were more supported in their explorations, certainly by the teacher, and sometimes, though not always, by each other. We were delighted to be able to document the children's work more closely. The vignettes also validated clay as a medium that could support young children's thinking. We noticed that clay became a "voice" for very young children as they tried to represent their ideas. We also recognized the critical role that teachers play in promoting that voice. For example, with Kimberly's scaffolding, the clay supported Collin's story of a joyful outing with his father. With Kimberly and Dee's support, Ethan's problem of hidden popcorn became a study of reversibility.

Kimberly's primary role was very evident in all the vignettes. She engaged in parallel play, expanded on the use of props, narrated the children's actions, and asked questions to clarify the children's meaning. As well as supporting the children's explorations, the small groupings also appeared to support

Kimberly's ability to be more attentive, more active in the children's inquiries. Like the children, Kimberly was fully engaged. We were beginning to realize that by documenting this experience we would inform our teaching while increasing our understanding of the children and the medium of clay.

Revisiting Our Questions

Our observations were deepening our understanding of our pedagogy, the children, and clay. We felt that we still had much to learn, however, from our small group encounters and made the decision to continue looking at small groupings of children exploring clay. While each exploration is worthy of lengthy discussion, we were particularly intrigued by the vignette that we documented in the next chapter. It gave us yet another opportunity to rethink children's co-construction of knowledge during toddlerhood.

Chapter 5
Collaborating with Clay & Each Other

Challenging Pedagogy

In the past, American early childhood educators have consistently underestimated the competence of young children (Bredekamp 1993). We have not often used words like *cooperation, concentration,* and *collaboration* when listing attributes of toddlers. However, these qualities develop on a continuum and are present in very young children. In a study entitled "The Beginnings of Collaboration in Peer Interaction," Verba argues, "The roots of basic peer interaction patterns reach back into infancy. The similarities across age levels suggest a functional continuity between the prelinguistic and linguistic periods of development" (1994, 125).

We found that our study also challenged the more traditional pedagogy of our profession and instead offered us images of very young children who were thoughtful and intentional. Our toddlers' ability to focus on their interests and meaningful questions was sustained by significant relationships and open-ended materials.

This study was not the first time we had witnessed these qualities in young children, but it was one of the first times we came to an investigation with a focus that was continually guided by our questions.

Continuing Our Small Group Study

We wanted to take a closer look at how toddler relationships might support their investigations with clay. This chapter looks once again at Natalie and Ethan, who had already spent more than a half hour working with clay before this vignette began. In this dialogue you will hear the voices of Natalie and Ethan as well as those of their teachers, whose interest and questions helped to sustain and clarify their exploration. We believe you will also observe two children who are deeply engaged in joint elaboration, which, as defined by Verba (1994), is goal-oriented, involves the sharing of meaning, and requires communicative strategies for involving and guiding the other's activity.

Driving the Car

Kimberly places a box of assorted open-ended tools out on the table. The tools have the potential to leave a variety of impressions in the clay. Ethan chooses a round piece of plastic about 5 inches in diameter and holds it up in the air with both hands. He twists it back and forth deliberately.

Ethan: "Drive the car."
Kimberly: "You're driving the car?"
Ethan: "Like this."

Ethan points to the front of a slab of clay. "This is my headlights. Like this."

Kimberly: "Like that?"

Natalie comes over to observe Ethan's car.

Natalie: "Where's the light?"

Ethan: "Right here." He pats the front of the clay.

Kimberly: "Ethan says this is the steering wheel and these are the lights."

Natalie: "Where? I'll need some. . . ." She goes to the box full of tools.

Dee: "Ethan, do you want to make some lights to go on the front?"

Ethan: "Yeah."

Dee: "Hmm. How can we do that? Can we make some lights?"

Natalie returns to Ethan's car with a blue tube. The end of the tube has spokes radiating out from a center circle.

Natalie: "I want to make one for you too."

Kimberly: "You're gonna make a light for Ethan?"

Natalie: "Okay. Light."

Thus Natalie enters Ethan's world. She offers to join him in his efforts to make lights for his car. An expert play partner, Natalie observes first, and then presses the tube into the clay.

Ethan: "Back here."

Natalie: "Right here?"

Ethan: "Uh huh."

Natalie: "See."

Ethan: "Right here."

Natalie: "Oh."

Natalie takes her cues from Ethan, making sure that she is interpreting his agenda correctly.

Dee: "Ethan wants a lot of lights on his car."

Ethan: "Right here." He points again to another area.

Natalie: "Okay." She pushes the tool to make another light.

Kimberly: "What else does your car need?"

Ethan: "Lots of lights!"

Kimberly: "Lots of lights."

Ethan points to the steering wheel.

Kimberly: "And a steering wheel. What else does a car need?"

Natalie: ". . . light!"

Ethan begins to push the tube into the clay as if he's making more lights.

Kimberly: "I wonder . . . uh . . . if the car needs some wheels?"

Ethan: "Why?" He begins to make marks with the tube on the side of the clay slab where wheels might go.

Natalie has gone to the box of tools again. She returns with a bristle block.

Natalie: "You need a block for your car, huh, Ethan?"

Ethan: "Yeah."

Natalie pushes the block into the clay, leaving its familiar marks.

Now she must have a new idea about the formation of the car. Natalie abandons the bristle block and lifts the steering wheel from the clay, but finds that she has gone too far!

Natalie: "I take this off?"

Ethan: "No!"

Ethan returns the wheel to the top of the clay car. He holds up the blue tool again that Natalie used to create lights.

Kimberly: "What can that be? Can that be part of the car?"

Ethan: "Yeah."

Kimberly: "What part?"

Ethan: "That a key for car."

Natalie: "What is that?"

Ethan: "That a key."

Kimberly: "It's a key for the car?"

Ethan: "Yeah."

Kimberly: "Where can you put it?"

Ethan: "Right here."

Ethan touches the pretend key to the side of the slab of clay.

Kimberly: "What else does your car need?"

Natalie: "Can we, um . . . um . . . need some . . ."

Ethan: "Cake."

Natalie: "Um . . . some . . . Chex? Some Chex!"

Ethan: "Uh . . ."

Kimberly is cutting a ball in half with the round tool used for slicing. Though Natalie appears to be engrossed in a discussion of food with Ethan, she must be observing Kimberly from the corner of her eye. She leaves Ethan's side and moves to the other side of Kimberly.

Natalie: "What are you doing?"

Kimberly: "I'm thinking about a way to make a tire. Could this be a tire?"

Ethan: "Yeah."

Kimberly: "Where would it go?"

Ethan: "Right here." He points to the back of the clay.

Kimberly: "You want to put it on?"

Ethan places the wheel on the back of the clay slab.

Ethan: "It's a van!"

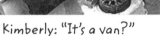

Kimberly: "It's a van?"

Ethan: "Yeah."

Kimberly: "Is that tire on the back?"

Ethan: "Yeah."

Kimberly: "That makes it a van?"

Ethan: "Yeah."

Natalie sticks a second "tire" on the back of Ethan's van. Once again she attempts to extend Ethan's play, but Ethan removes her addition immediately.

Kimberly: "Where would that one go?"

Ethan: "Right here." He places the "tire" on the table.

Kimberly: "Right here? It doesn't need to go on the van?"

Ethan: "Yeah."

Kimberly: "It just needs a tire on the back?"

Ethan: "Yeah. Has . . . right here." Ethan runs his finger around the edge of the clay.

Kimberly: "It has lots of lights and it has a steering wheel and it has a tire on the back. Does it need anything else?"

Natalie: "Does it need a . . . does it need a line?"

Ethan: "Yeah!"

Natalie: "I'll get it!" She goes to the other side of the table and grabs another tool.

Kimberly: "A line? What kind of a line does the car need?"

Natalie: "Green."

Kimberly: "A green line?"

Where does the idea of a line come from here? When Ethan runs his finger around the edge of the clay does it remind Natalie of a line? Certainly Natalie has some knowledge of the fact that cars can be painted with lines.

Natalie notices Kimberly cutting the clay.

Natalie: "What are you cutting with?"

Kimberly: "What am I cutting with? I'm using this."

Natalie takes the tool Kimberly has been using and begins to make a slicing motion at a ball of clay.

Dee: "Are you thinking you're going to use that to make a line?"

Ethan: "Yeah." Ethan points to a clay light. "It's a button. It's going!"

Kimberly and Dee are watching Natalie cut. They miss Ethan's statement about the light becoming a button, and it goes unacknowledged.

Natalie: "I'll put one right here." (Referring to the line.)

Ethan places another half ball on the back of the van.

Ethan: "Two, two, two, two tires!"

Kimberly: "Two tires?"

Ethan: "Yeah."

The dialogue temporarily slides into a discussion of food again as the half balls become "bagels." The children pause and seem to regroup their thoughts. Natalie starts to attach the half ball to the back of the van.

Natalie: "Where'd my other piece go?"

Ethan: "Here." He points to the table.

Natalie: "Oh."

Kimberly: "What are you going to do with those?"

Natalie: "I need . . ."

Ethan: "No, this one."

Natalie places the half ball on the back of the van.

Natalie: " 'Nother light."

Kimberly: "Oh. Those are lights now?"

Natalie nods her head yes.

Natalie: "Where the lights?"

Kimberly: "Where are the lights?"

Natalie: "What are these?" Natalie pokes her fingers at the original marks she made for the lights.

Kimberly: "Do you remember how they got there?"

Ethan grabs the tube that Natalie used to make the "light" marks. " 'Nother one!" He stamps more "lights" onto the surface of the clay as Natalie watches.

With this statement we find Ethan embracing Natalie's original idea of how to produce "lights." He stamps the "light" pattern on the clay form multiple times.

Kimberly: "Okay. What do you need?"

Natalie: "This." She goes to the other side of the table and holds up a clay tool.

Kimberly: "What do you think you can do with that one?"

Natalie: "This is a sharp one."

Kimberly: "That is a sharp one."

Ethan tries to take the tool from Natalie's hand. "I same one," he says, reaching for the bucket of tools.

Kimberly: "You found another."

The children poke at the slab with various tools from the bucket.

Kimberly: "Is this still a car, or is it something different?" There is no response. "Can you tell me something about the parts you're putting on? What will that part do?"

Interest in the car dialogue is fading. Ethan begins a game of tossing tools into the bucket that Natalie has placed on the floor next to Ethan.

Reflecting on the Observation This clay story revealed many aspects of the children's thinking and the significance of a medium that has a memory, is transformable, and offers the possibility of representing objects, ideas, or events. A circular plastic form that was presented alongside the clay seemed to prompt Ethan's actions and words, and he informed us that he was pretending to drive a car. Almost immediately Natalie became a collaborative partner in this story, offering her ideas and helping to shape the plot. The story was fluid, even if the main idea strayed from time to time. As the plot unfolded, we found Ethan accepting Natalie's suggestions on most occasions and incorporating her vision into the story line. However, if the plot strayed too far from his thinking, Ethan was quick to reject Natalie's idea, as when Natalie tried to remove the wheel from the car.

The narrative also rang true to the children's life experiences, evident when Natalie suggested that they needed food. Kimberly knew that eating food in the car was an important ritual for the children on their long drives to and from school, and so, to the insider, this was a perfectly delightful acknowledgment of the significant role that food plays when riding in a car.

This vignette sheds light on both the individual child's competence as meaning-maker and on the nature of toddlerhood in general. The children's story captured not just cooperative play, but went beyond cooperation to reflect these toddlers' abilities to negotiate a shared script. Although the reciprocity was limited in scope (we did not see a neatly packaged exchange of ideas), each toddler contributed to the play, and each toddler altered his or her ideas according to the actions or suggestions of the other.

Listening closely to the words and the body language of these two young children prompted us to rethink their cognitive processes as they negotiated shared meaning through social interactions. Philippe Rochat (2001) would describe their interactions as demonstrating secondary intersubjectivity in that Natalie and Ethan understood that they were jointly attending to a common object or script. They often took interest in each other's ideas and used these to advance the plot. The dialogue remained fluid, and even when the children's contributions diverged, the joint story always resurfaced. For example, as Natalie pursued making a line (both children seemed to know about decorative lines on cars), Ethan was discussing the tires on the back of the car. The shared script temporarily split into two directions, but merged again when Natalie asked Kimberly about the marks that were lights. Ethan assimilated the idea by grabbing the tool Natalie originally used to make lights, and stamped more lights into the clay. Ethan and Natalie were like soul mates, indeed having spent much of their young life together. Each enjoyed the other's company; each was tolerant and respectful of the other's theories.

Within this story we hear the support of their teacher. She was truly present. She clarified their simple words, asked for confirmation of her understanding, offered questions that helped to sustain the dialogue, and occasionally participated in parallel play alongside the children. Having a primary teacher who was intimately familiar with the children played a crucial role in sustaining the children's explorations. Kimberly had a history with these children going back to infancy, and the stability she brought to these sessions cannot be underestimated. She was passionate about her work with these children, and she was deeply interested in understanding how they explored the clay.

Reflecting on Our Small Group Sessions

Natalie and Ethan's experience was one of six small group sessions, all similarly rich and varied. Some were very collaborative in nature, while others relied more on the teacher's skills. Looking back over the scripts, we wondered about the factors that might be significant in sustaining the children's clay investigations. How much of their attention was due to the small groupings? To the teacher's focus? To the way we presented the clay?

We also wondered how the tools affected the children's exploration. In particular, what role did the tools play in creating the emerging representational scripts we were beginning to see? After reviewing several small group sessions we observed that the children's use of tools seemed to support their scripts on many occasions. Ethan's use of the rolling pin during the popcorn investigation, Collin's use of a dump truck, Eric's use of dowels and cutters, and Ethan and Natalie's use of tools to create the car script led us to question how much the addition of tools helped us know the children's intent. We also questioned the types of tools we were providing and wondered if we should begin to offer more authentic clay tools.

In retrospect, we probably should have begun our investigation with no tools. Certainly we could then have been more thoughtful about the role of tools and intentional about when to introduce them. In fact, during some of the last clay sessions we presented the clay without tools. The absence of tools did not limit the children's exploration, though they did ask for them several times. Without tools the children also seemed to move more rapidly from script to script. Possibly the tools would have supported or extended their use of clay. Looking back, it seems clear to us that the availability of tools made it possible for these very young children to use clay to represent their ideas in a way that was possibly more satisfying to them and more visible to us.

Looking to the Future

As teachers we were nearing the end of this investigation, but the children's explorations with clay were not done. The final chapter in this book is a reflection on the children's use of clay in the preschool, an "epilogue" if you will. Before closing this book with stories of Collin, Natalie, Andrew, Ethan, Maria, Erik, and Joey as preschoolers, however, we offer the following chapter that describes the experiences of another group of children who were introduced to clay as infants. Their teachers motivated us to consider the use of clay with children as young as seven months. The teachers explored alternative strategies for documenting, and reexamined both the role of the teacher and the role of tools in supporting children's exploration of clay. Their courage inspired us to share this work-in-progress with you.

References

Bredekamp, Sue. 1993. Reflections on Reggio Emilia. *Young Children* 49: 13–17.

Rochat, Philippe. 2001. *The infant's world.* Cambridge: Harvard University Press.

Verba, Mina. 1994. The beginnings of collaboration in peer interaction. *Human Development* 37: 125–139.

Chapter 6
New Beginnings

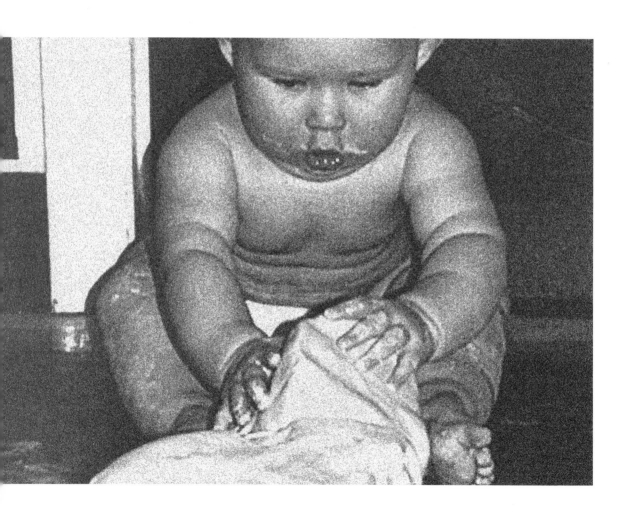

Beginning with Ourselves

It was February and the staff gathered for our weekly meeting. We had decided that this semester we would read two books, Louise Boyd Cadwell's new book, *Bringing Learning to Life: The Reggio Approach to Early Childhood Education* (2003), and later *The Geography of Childhood: Why Children Need Wild Places* by Gary Nabhan and Stephen Trimble (1994). Between reading those two books our entire staff would have the rare opportunity to travel together to Reggio Emilia, a trip for which we had raised funds during the previous three years.

The facilitator for this staff meeting was Heather, a new teacher in the toddler room, though familiar to us as a student from years past. She began the meeting in a manner that we had agreed upon this semester—we each write for approximately fifteen minutes about a topic or idea the facilitator proposes. On several occasions this semester, facilitators asked us to write about personal experiences from our childhood. Following this model, Heather asked us to write and share our recollections of our childhood experiences using various media. Our memories varied along a continuum from little experience to rich histories with media such as watercolors, clay, and sewing. We were surprised when Heather's co-teacher Amanda described her youthful experiences. She shared her writing with us.

> As a very young child I was a "drawer"—crayons, marker, pen. I drew all the time. In church and in restaurants I decorated menus and bulletins. I loved that ink and crayon and marker stayed right where you put them on the page. I did a lot of tracing and coloring in coloring books. I was very much mesmerized by the challenge of aiming for perfection and being as competent as adults. In middle school and high school I was very drawn to three dimensions more often than not. I couldn't translate my ideas or contain them to a flat surface. I created large mixed-media collages, lamps, and little wire sculptures. Clay was always soothing and relaxing. I used clay a great deal but not for representing. I loved making real things.

Now a toddler teacher, Amanda had, in fact, been exploring clay with the children since they were infants. We now realized that her eagerness to explore this medium with babies was shaped by her own personal history and experience.

In this chapter we share some small but significant developments as Amanda and a small group of children explored clay as infants and toddlers. What we offer is by no means a complete chronicle of their experiences. These children are still very interested in clay, and use it on almost a daily basis. We make no attempt to summarize the totality of this experience. We are still living it. We think, however, that you may find differences in the choices we now make in supporting the children's investigations with this medium, differences that are explained by our history, the children, their teachers, and our altered environment. We are especially indebted to Amanda Terreri for her contributions to this chapter.

Amanda, her co-teacher, and Dee made a plan to present clay to the infants. They wanted to be able to document this session closely so they decided that one person would video-tape, one would take slides, and Amanda would support the infants' interactions with clay. Amanda was unsure about how and where to present the clay. Eventually we decided to use the

small kitchen space inside the infant class-room area, a familiar yet relatively open space. The floor was carefully prepared for the children's interactions with the clay by taping paper over the linoleum. For the remainder of the semester, this setup signaled to the babies that it was time to explore clay.

• • •

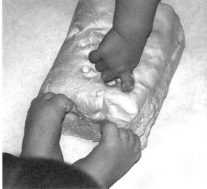

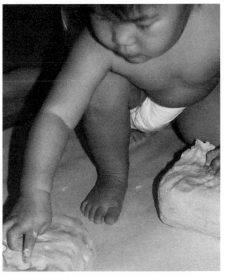

Touching the clay with various parts of their bodies marks the beginning of new relationships. The children use both hands and feet as they explore this new medium. They quickly go from reaching with an open hand to the classic extended pointer finger. They show not only that they grasp the trans-formational qualities of this medium, but also an under-standing of their finger's usefulness as a probe. These begin-ning probes help the children acquire information about this

substance, as when Kailey places her finger inside a hole Amanda has made.

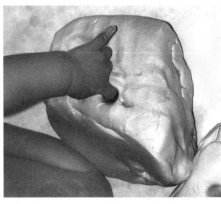

Maddie's close exploration of the clay follows her persistence at rolling the clay closer to her body. She leans way over in order to use her mouth to explore the clay's properties. In her efforts to gain as much information as possible, she gets so close that the clay leaves traces all over her body that attest to both her strength and her level of engagement.

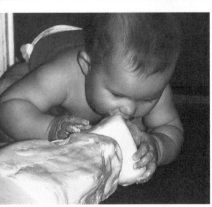

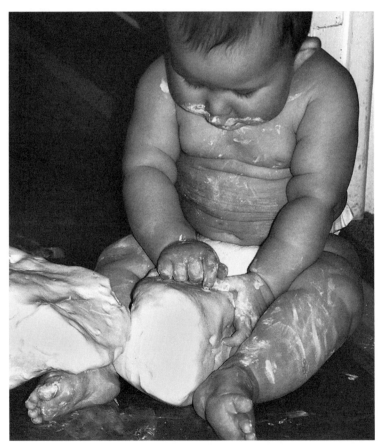

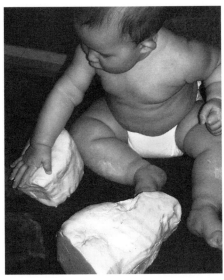

Kailey uses Amanda's finger to make deep holes. Kailey's method of exploration, asking directly for adult assistance, is familiar to Amanda. Their history together assures Amanda that Kailey will soon be exploring clay on her own.

Reflecting on this action in her notes, Amanda writes, "When Kailey takes my finger and we poke together I am moved. We are truly sharing this experience, sharing competencies. She understands that I value her request and follow the directions, her cues she gives me. I have two ideas: the clay is difficult to poke so she uses my finger as a tool, knowing that it works; she is unsure and experiences the clay first through me, then she tries it. She is very clear about what she wants me to do and exactly where my fingers should go. I think we both feel a sense of relief in understanding each other."

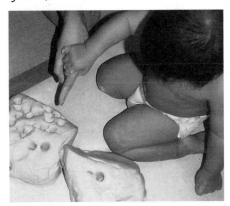

Sean has Amanda's full attention as he begins his first exploration of clay. He finds humor and joy in these first moments of interactions as he watches Amanda poke the clay.

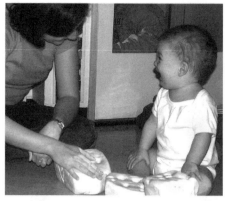

On this day, the infants' explorations with clay produce unexpected events. Mason has never stood without support. Nevertheless, he eagerly bobs up to a standing position and back down again, sharing the excitement of a small piece of clay with Amanda.

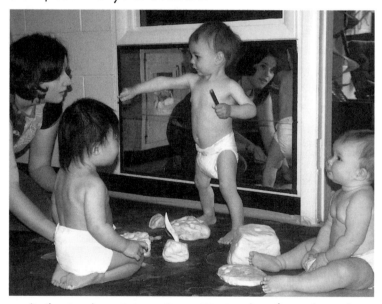

Kailey has been interacting with the clay, Amanda, and her peers for about twenty minutes. She crawls to another teacher who has been videotaping the children's interactions with clay. Kailey insists on showing her clay to the teacher behind the camera. The teacher sets the camera down and lowers herself to the ground. Kailey shares her balls of clay and is clearly excited about this exchange. Kailey then uses her teacher's body as a support to stand, turns around, and walks off.

We are surprised by Kailey's actions, which seem to happen with such ease. Kailey has never walked at school, and we find out later she has never walked at home. We had all known for some time that Kailey had excellent balance, and could no

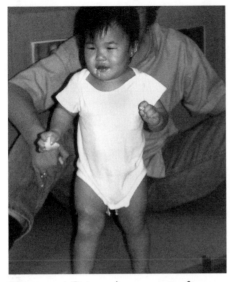

doubt walk if she were to try. We note that she has chosen this moment to exercise her increased mobility. Kailey is a cautious child, who closely observes others and thinks carefully about all her actions. We cannot know why this is the moment she chooses to walk, but we reflect on the circumstances around this event. It is a close, quiet afternoon in the infant room; only three children are awake. All the children are in the kitchen, interacting with each other, their mentor teachers, and the clay. The children are becoming familiar with the clay. It is a medium that we suspect they associate with attention, warmth, freedom of exploration, surprise, challenge, and joy. It is a safe environment that has the potential to create unexpected opportunities.

The desire to use tools is also evident from the children's first sessions with clay. They aid the children in poking and at times, seem to sustain their inquiries. Tools give the children different information than their fingers do. Some tools

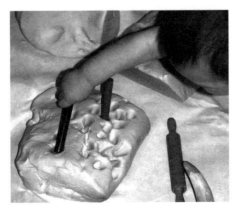

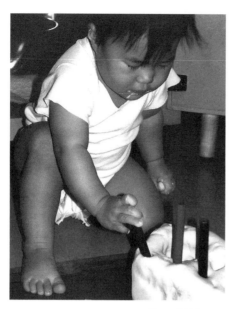

can be easier to insert in clay than fingers. Sometimes tools resist being separated from the clay. The angle of extraction is important to the children's growing knowledge about the medium.

In her notes Amanda includes her thinking about tools. "Originally I intended not to use tools, to let them experience [clay] with their bodies first. However, this incorporation of other materials helped sustain the interaction."

Reflecting on the Observations As we looked back over these vignettes we realized that these stories reflected both our context and our values. First, we were quite sure that the quality of investment by Amanda both in the children and the medium was the single most important factor in introducing the clay to the infants. The infants' desire to know the clay could not be separated from their need to explore in a safe context with an adult whom they trusted. Everything that happens to young children, and especially infants and toddlers, happens in the context of relationships. The quality of the relationships sets the context for the babies' investigations and either invites or discourages risk taking. Although both Amanda and the babies entered into the investigation with some hesitation, together they were willing to take risks.

After the first presentation, Amanda's notes reflected her uncertainty about how to set up the clay for these children. She wrote, "How big? How small? More than one piece? Knowing that this matters but not sure what the outcome will be for each. Flexibility seems to be the answer; adapting to needs of multiple children . . . more pieces." The babies referred to Amanda and to each other throughout the first sessions. As their comfort level increased, we saw them taking risks, possibly in several ways, but most dramatically with their motor skills.

Second, as we looked over the images we had of the infant's explorations with clay we were particularly interested in the extent to which Maddie used her whole body to experience the clay. At seven months, she was the youngest child to be investigating the medium. We believed that whole-body explorations of a material such as clay might provide information that is quite different from being exposed to it at a later age. In this case, Maddie's body was covered with traces of clay, no doubt giving her a unique sensation as it dried on her skin. She was immersed in the clay, a full-blown sensorimotor experience that she might never experience again. (We should pause here to note that the traces of clay around her mouth were the result of brief contact while mouthing the clay, not because she was eating it. If mouthing clay had been prolonged or her primary means for gaining information about the medium, we would have made the choice to wait a little while before offering the clay to her. The traces left around her mouth are due to the very soft nature of porcelain clay.)

Inviting the children to experience the clay with their whole bodies is second nature to the culture of our program. For as long as our program has existed, our youngest children have explored materials in the freedom of relatively little clothing. Our babies and toddlers are frequently found exploring media such as paint, dressed only in their diapers. It was brought to our attention recently, however, that this is not a universal practice. We had the opportunity while in Italy to share a few of our clay images with teachers in Pistoia, and they in turn shared images of their children painting. It was a delightful exchange with an unexpected twist for us. As pictures of our babies were shown exploring the clay in diapers, our colleagues in Pistoia expressed surprise that our young children had little clothing on. It is not a practice they share in Italy, where we were told parents are very concerned with their children staying warm. They asked us why our children were in their diapers. We were so surprised by this question, that it was a few seconds before we began to give a rationale to our practice! The question pushed us to think through this practice that we had long taken for granted. We want the children to have the freedom to explore with their whole bodies; to have a sensory experience that we believe complements their development. Perhaps the fact that we live in Vermont, where the winters can be long and harsh is a partial explanation as well. Are we trying to create an indoor atmosphere to recall the freedom of summer— freedom from cold, freedom from snowsuits, freedom of mobility? Perhaps it is our way of thumbing our nose at winter!

The Infants Become Toddlers: New Clay Observations

There was a brief hiatus of several months in the children's engagement with clay. Because summers in Vermont are a time to relish the outdoors, over the past few years our center has seen the youngest children away from their classrooms and out on campus and in the larger Burlington community. With fall, the weather was getting colder. The clay was once again presented as the children were spending more time in their classroom. They repeated many of their earlier explorations with the clay such as poking, patting, and pinching. These children had a history with clay. They knew a lot about the physical properties of the medium. They had come to understand that the shape of clay can be transformed and that their actions with clay create traces of remembrance. They knew what clay feels like, what clay tastes like. The children had grown a lot over the summer; their balance had improved as well as their strength. Most of the children were now walking. Socially we saw small rituals and toddler jokes emerge; they were more in harmony with their peers. We noticed several significant developments in their clay explorations as well.

Over the summer we had observed games of appearance and disappearance and turn taking that involved countless materials and spaces encountered by the toddlers. Now these games were extended to the clay. We believe the following vignettes relate to these emerging games.

Clay Games

Amanda makes a few circles from coils of clay. Kailey is very interested in this form. Holding the circle to her eye, she uses the form to play peek-a-boo with others. When a larger circle is created, Kailey combines it with a stick to investigate the relationship between the circle and the stick. First she places the

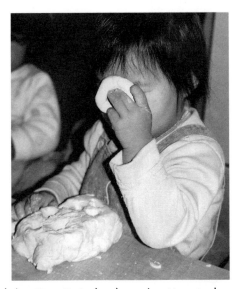

stick in the circle. She slides the stick slowly under the circle, peering in to observe its appearance in the center of the circle. Slowly she slides the stick out of the circle. Kailey repeats her actions multiple times, possibly confirming her hypothesis about the relationship of the stick to the circle. To us it seems

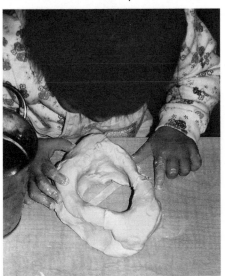

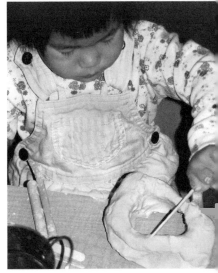

to be similar to the game of peek-a-boo we so often see in the classroom.

Several weeks later the teachers present porcelain and terra-cotta clay to the children in various forms. The children have been interacting with the clay and their peers for over a half hour, and their interest is beginning to fade. The teachers decide to take the children to the gym, but Tessa is more interested in staying with the clay. She stays in the classroom with Amanda and proceeds to explore the clay. Tessa is

most interested in the round balls of clay and how these combine with a plastic cup. Tessa begins a self-initiated game of peek-a-boo with a ball of clay. She places the cup over the ball and looks to Amanda. "Where is?" Tessa asks. She lifts the cup and exclaims, "Here is!" She repeats the sequence over and over, trying out various balls of clay. It is clear that Tessa places value on this exploration. It is one she engages in for over fifteen minutes. The environment is familiar and she has Amanda's undivided attention. She checks in with Amanda frequently as if confirming that Amanda values this game.

In a social game of weight Maddie initiates play with Kailey involving a large mass of clay. Although uncertain at first, Kailey calculates that Maddie is pushing the clay toward her in fun. A game of turn-taking ensues with the clay being pushed back and forth.

The toddlers also use the large masses of clay to explore their bodies' ability to balance. Time and time again the toddlers perch on the large clumps of clay to practice this skill.

Aishu climbs on top of the clay while Amanda "spots" from behind.

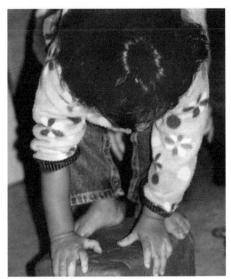

Tessa is thrilled by her ability to stand on top of the clay! Elias secures his position by digging his toes into the clay.

Mason finds the large mass of clay just right for sitting. Tessa wants to join him!

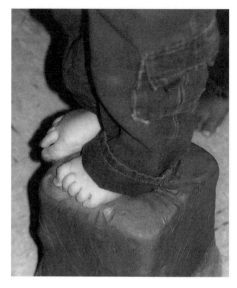

Reflecting on the Observations Throughout the fall months the children had the opportunity to explore the clay in different forms. Sometimes the clay was presented as a large mass. Other times balls, coils, and slabs were offered. These variations had a definite impact on the children's explorations, as we saw in the game between Kailey and Maddie. Their game was both funny and challenging at the same time, and it could not have happened with small pieces of clay.

Real Work: Cutting the Clay

During a clay session in November, Amanda uses wire wrapped around two small handles to cut through the clay. The chil-

dren observe this with great interest and begin to work dili- gently to accomplish this task themselves. Whole clay sessions become devoted to the single goal of slic- ing through the clay.

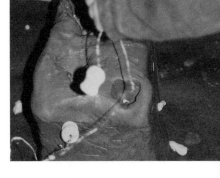

The children take this challenge seriously. They seem to under- stand that this is "real" work. Throughout the first sessions the chil-

dren are solely interested in the act of slicing. At first they put the tool on top of the clay to try it out. The resulting small pieces of clay are left neglected, as if they are unimportant.

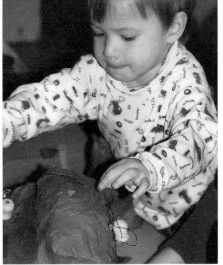

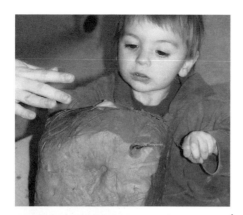

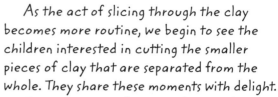

As the act of slicing through the clay becomes more routine, we begin to see the children interested in cutting the smaller pieces of clay that are separated from the whole. They share these moments with delight.

The seriousness of their endeavor also begins to take on a lighter side, maybe even a bit of humor. This is especially evident when the children finally slice through a large piece of clay. They put so much strength into pulling on the wire that their efforts often result in a temporary loss of balance when the clay is completely cut. Squeals of joy can be heard as they accomplish the goal of pulling the wire through the heavy mass of clay, losing their balance, but quickly regaining it. This accomplishment is often accompanied by a little dance!

Caring for the Clay We watched as the children slowly began to assume nurturing roles in the classroom. They had shown a sense of empathy for nonliving as well as living things. They relished the opportunity to do "real work," work which was authentic and meaningful. They had been caring for the birds outside their classroom window, planting and caring for tomato seeds, sweeping the floor and wiping down tables, and offering comfort to their peers who were distressed. In short, they were developing a sense of other in relationship to self. Consequently they could now share the nurturing that they had received. The children were now transferring these empathetic behaviors to the clay.

• • •

The children stand over the clay and anticipate the problem facing them. They understand that the clay is a material that needs to be cared for. They have watched and listened as their teachers have modeled wrapping up the clay at the end of each encounter so it stays moist and pliable. Now the children show us they are ready to participate in this ritual.

Elias begins with Amanda's help. Amanda tells him that she too struggles with the large pieces of clay. "Elias, sometimes I find it helpful to first roll it on its side." Together they struggle with placing the bag over the clay. When the clay is safely in the bag, Elias shows us he knows the job is not complete. He takes the open end of the bag and begins to roll it together, securing the clay from the air.

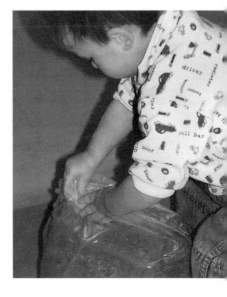

The Desire to Make Shapes *(The following observations and discussion are based on documents written by teacher Amanda Terreri and early childhood student Lyndsay O'Neill.)*

The toddlers have been increasingly interested in shaping the clay. They have been interested in the shape they call "snake," which is a small coil of clay. By watching their teachers they understand that to produce this shape you must take a piece of clay between your palms and rub your hands back and forth. They are also very interested in "balls." However, the subtle difference in hand movements needed to produce a ball is neither easy to understand nor easy to master. An example of this challenge comes from an observation written by Lyndsay: "Mason is rolling a piece of clay in his hands. He says, 'I make a ball.' He keeps rolling and then takes the piece out of his hand and gasps, 'A snake!' I say, 'You thought it would be a ball, but the way you moved your hands made a snake.'"

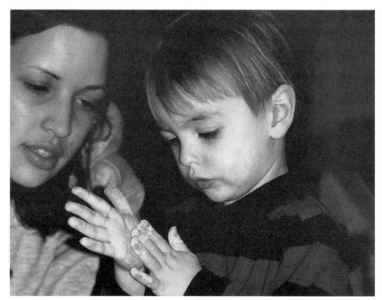

Sharing Our Observations Amanda and Lyndsay had been watching the children's efforts for a few weeks. The children were on the verge of discovering how to make a ball and the teachers had also noticed that they were trying to learn from each other. Amanda and Lyndsay decided to try a new format for their observations that they had seen in *Making Learning Visible* (Giudici et al. 2001), a book about the process of documentation and small group experiences from the schools in Reggio Emilia, Italy. They wished to capture the essence of the emerging conversations between these very young children, and how their actions and words influenced each other. Amanda and Lyndsay created a chart with columns *(see below)*. A child or teacher's name was on the top of each column. As they transcribed the conversations from the audiotapes, they captured the collaborative nature of the session by spacing each person's response on a new line. This created a chronology of each person's comments within the flow of the conversation.

Lyndsay	Aishu	Mason	Amanda
		Here.	
Thanks.			
		Here you go.	
Thank you, I'll put it back in the container in case someone wants to use it.			
		Here. Back in 'tainer. I hold it.	
Those wires are very bendy.			
	rhyming sounds (? bendy bendy...) Piece? Ball?	Make a piece.	
You want a ball? Can you make one?	Yeah!		
You can make one? I think Mason knows how to make one, maybe he can show you. Mason can you show Aishu how to make a ball?	Yeah.		
		Yeah.	

(continued on next page)

Lyndsay	Aishu	Mason	Amanda
He is making one. He is rolling it in his hand. He broke off a little piece.	Piece.		
Maybe you can take a piece off this clay and roll it in between your hands to make a ball.		Make a snake.	
You made a snake.	Masey. (A makey dat?)		
He made a snake. Look at he is using his finger to pull little pieces off the clay to make snakes.	Piece? A dat Masey yeah?	Yeah. Make a snake.	
That's a small snake.		? . . . need a water. I (need) water.	
	(Asking something about snake) da me snake. Me snake? Yeah. A ball.		
You want to make a ball? Mason can you show her how to make a ball? Can you show her? She wants to make one.		Like dat.	
Like that. He's showing you how. Yeah. Here you can break a piece off. You can dig it to break a piece off.		Uh mine.	
Oh look, there's a piece.	Piece.		
OK, now what do you do?			

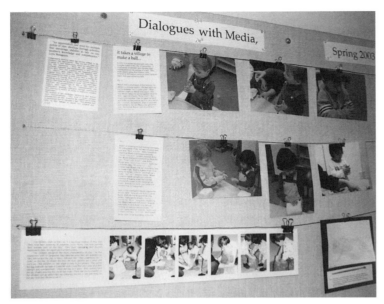

Amanda and Lyndsay decided to share their documentation of the rich conversations among the children with our larger community. Lyndsay introduced the children's work, displaying a series of small documents along with photographs in the hallway outside the toddler room.

Here are excerpts from the text of the display:

Collaboration among peers has become evident in the children's clay explorations. They are full of ideas and invention in their interactions, which are revisited with each clay experience. Each day the children are producing sequences and developments in their actions, which have their own practical and imaginative path. They observe each other's ideas and methods, and integrate them into their clay explorations. They understand the value of their peers' ideas as well as the importance of sharing their own perspectives. This is becoming more and more evident as the children begin to express their ideas and feelings in words. They share ideas, questions, and perspectives as well as their desire to support each other. We see communication and collaborative thinking cultivated through experiences that embrace a variety of media to represent common experiences.

The medium of clay challenges children as they become more representational. They work to create common meaning with the clay. Presently the toddlers are working to understand how to represent a ball. They scaffold each other as they attempt to master this common goal.

It Takes a Village to Make a Ball

A story or a puzzle has emerged within the complex layers of the clay investigation. A small group of children have focused their collaboration on making a ball. They work closely using their fingers, tools, innovative techniques, and each other's help to reach their goal of making balls.

Day 1 Mason rolls a small piece of clay between his palms in a circular motion. His face lights up and he screams, "Ball! I make a ball." Elias watches closely as Mason tries again. This time Mason keeps his hands together while he rolls. Again he shouts, "Make a ball!" But, much to his surprise when he opens his hand and holds out the piece of clay it is not a ball at all. "A snake," he explains. Elias is surprised and excited by the skill Mason has presented him. He mimics Mason's actions and says, "Make a snake too."

Day 2 Mason is reexamining his ball-making techniques. He rolls a piece of clay between his palms and says, "Make a snake!" Aishu is carefully observing Mason's techniques and asks, "Masey make dat?" Lyndsay reminds Aishu that Mason first pulls a piece of clay from the slab, "Piece a dat Masey?" asks Aishu. Mason says, "Yeah, make a snake." Aishu has a different idea, "Me snake? No, a ball." Lyndsay asks Mason if he can show Aishu how he makes a ball. Rolling a piece of clay in his palms he replies, "Like dat," and holds up a snake. "Ball, Ball!" exclaims Aishu. Mason moves his hands up and down with the intention of making a ball, but with the outcome of a snake! A new challenge has arisen. How do you move your hands in a different way to make a ball?

Later in the investigation Kailey approaches the clay table. Amanda asks Aishu to show Kailey what she was doing with the clay earlier. Aishu gladly accepts. "Kailey. Showed me, Masey," says Aishu, explaining that Mason had shown her earlier. Amanda asks Aishu to show Kailey how she was working on making a ball and a snake. "No, snake," Aishu reminds Amanda. Aishu turns to Kailey and says, "Feel, soft," sharing with Kailey some of her knowledge of the clay.

Day 3 There has been a development in the ball-making exploration. Elias has discovered a new way to make a snake. He begins by rolling a piece of clay in his palms. "Making snake," he tells Aishu. He carefully places the snake on the table. "Hi snake!" he exclaims and gently places his hand on the snake. He begins to roll

and breaks off another piece to roll on the table. He diligently moves his hand up and down on the piece of clay. As he lifts his hand, he unveils another long, skinny snake. "Whoo! More 'nakes!'" Lyndsay brings Elias' newly found technique to Aishu's attention. She begins to carefully observe, her eyes locked on Elias's hands. She places her hand on a piece of clay and begins to roll it up and down. "Ball, ball," she says. When she removes her hand she gasps. What a predicament!

Elias is still practicing his new snake-making style. He is proud of his discovery, and he shares his work with Amanda. "Made dat Manda. Made dat Manda!" he announces as he holds his snakes high in the air.

his hand back and forth over the snake. When he lifts his hand he reveals a long skinny snake! "Make 'nakes!" he cheers

Reflecting on the Children's Dialogue In this series of vignettes recorded by the teachers, we found children supporting each other as they focused on learning the process of ball making. They were gently guided in this endeavor by their student teacher, Lyndsay, who sometimes loaned information to the children, sometimes referred them to each other, sometimes clarified their words or actions, and sometimes refrained from participating in the dialogue. The balance is delicate. The decision to intervene or not intervene, as well as how to intervene, is particularly difficult for a new teacher. We know, however, that all teachers struggle with these decisions on a daily basis. What is important is that teachers listen closely to the children and make deliberate choices about how to prepare the environment, what materials to offer children and how to present them, and how to interact with the children—all the elements of a teacher's practice—based on their knowledge of them. Lyndsay and her mentor-teacher, Amanda, documented the experiences and revisited both visual and auditory records for the purpose of trying to understand the children's interest and their questions. Reworking their documents for the purpose of making them public, they invited others to reflect on the children's work. How the teachers continue to present the clay and the roles they will take in future encounters are contingent upon their ongoing dialogues and interpretations of the children's questions.

Final Reflections

The stories in this book say as much, if not more, about the nature of our program as they do about how very young children come to know and use the medium of clay. That is how it should be. Our values, and more pragmatically, the organizational systems of our program motivated and scaffolded this experience. Like others who came before it and those who will follow, this investigation reinforces our value of teachers as researchers and lifelong learners.

Our initial investigation of toddlers and clay underscored the value and benefits of providing children the opportunity to work together in small groups and contributed to a growing belief that the center needed a studio space. It was no small decision on the part of the teachers to give up their staff room in order to create a space where small groups of children could have uninterrupted time to work together. The studio plays a significant role in the afterword, as it picks up where chapter 5 left off: with our protagonists, now preschoolers, artisans and artists whose medium is clay.

References
················

Cadwell, Louise Boyd. 2003. *Bringing learning to life:
      The Reggio approach to early childhood education.*
      New York: Teachers College Press.

Giudici, Claudia, Carla Rinaldi, and Mara Krechevsky (eds.)
      2001. *Making learning visible: Children as individual and
      group learners.* Reggio Emilia, Italy: Reggio Children.

Nabhan, Gary, and Stephen Trimble. 1994. *The geography
      of childhood: Why children need wild places.* Boston:
      Beacon Press.

Afterword

Barbara Burrington

The children you have met in this book grew up with clay in their lives. At school they encountered clay nearly everyday. They saw older children using clay, they walked by the Campus

Pottery Cooperative on their daily outings, they saw the work of potters and sculptors displayed in the campus gallery, and they viewed it on the shelves that line the clay studio, where we get fresh clay. These children understood that their teachers valued their early explorations with clay. The environment reflected their experiences with displays of photographs alongside printed words. Clay offered the children the possibility to research

their own questions and learn a new language, a symbolic language made up of processes and transformations.

Classrooms have a culture that rests in a larger context of systems and values, expectations, and complexities. In these stories many of the values that define the particular context are evident. One value recognizable in these images and anecdotes is that of time: time for observing life, time for entering play, time for building relationships, and time for revisiting ideas

and experiences. It takes a long time to learn to use tools and to understand media. No person is born knowing how to draw or write, how to move a paintbrush or dance or write music. No child enters the classroom asking to represent their thinking and state their questions with clay either. It takes time. And it takes teachers who honor that way of being with children—teachers who strive to enter the natural time frame of children.

Teachers have to make decisions. Dee and Kimberly made a decision to introduce a group of very young children to clay. They made a decision to observe the children with clay and with one another. Why did they put themselves on the line by going off in a new direction with toddlers? Why would teachers make such a risky choice? I believe their choice was based on the point of view and image they have of children. When teachers look at the group of children in their classroom and see possibilities, when they make decisions based on what children can do, they invite engagement, joy, and wonder into the classroom.

The overarching attitude that guides such innovation is one of research and inquiry. The world is not passively perceived and known. Integral to the process of learning is the active manipulation of our environment, right from the start! John Dewey made the point that feelings, hypotheses, and ideas mediate our encounters in the world only in the context of active inquiry.

How is this related to the clay study? Dee and Kimberly could have simply provided the toddlers with objects, toys, and materials that would have allowed them to do what they knew toddlers do: fill and empty; lift, carry, and move objects; touch various surfaces; exert force on things; and so on. What they did instead was make a qualitative distinction between immediate and structured events and objects, and a social situation, where the children, through experimentation, collaboration, concentrated efforts, and intentional actions, could use clay as a means to a richer end.

And yet, the richer end isn't actually an end at all, but rather an understanding or a series of large understandings. I worked with Andrew, Erik, Natalie, Collin, Maria, Ethan, and Joey when they were preschoolers. As preschoolers they could choose clay as a means to express, represent, and communicate their thinking. They knew clay. They knew how much force to exert when pushing or rolling it into a slab; how to exert pressure on two sides to make it move up; how to score clay and make slip in order to join pieces of clay together; how to roll coils and balls; how to use their fingers, fists, and thumbs as tools; how to pull protuberances; how to combine clay with other media; how to rejoin broken clay; and how to smooth clay with water. During the years I spent with these seven children, they continually chose clay as a medium.

The children depicted with clay what they held most dear. Small animals, bird nests, flower signs for the garden planters, birdbaths, a playground for their beloved hermit crabs, and

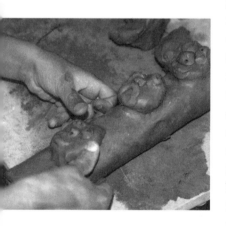

people, all of which reflects their growing understanding of their role as stewards of the natural world. They created gifts for special people and occasions, such as hockey games, playground equipment, totems depicting their stories, masks reflecting their identities, and shelters from places they could only imagine—India, Russia, Africa, Asia, and the American Southwest. Their shelters reflected their skill with clay, but more important, their understanding of places as areas of meaning and of the meaning shelter has for all people. The beauty of everything they made with clay resided in the process, the underlying concepts, and the communication of ideas and culture.

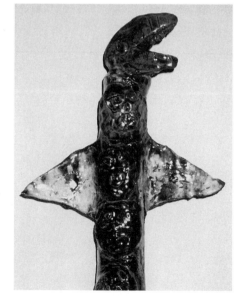

Their hockey rink, complete with players, pucks, benches, lines, and a Zamboni, is a coveted game among the current preschoolers. They know that children who came before them created it. They recognize the work and passion that were united to create this model of a much loved game. Examples of their work fill the  shelves of our little studio and inspire us today.

Who is more fortunate, the children who know clay well enough to use it as a form of expression and representation, or me? I get to teach in a school where children are given respect for their competence, potentials, and ideas; where there are no limits to knowing life's complexities; and where value is given to states of wonder, curiosity, imagination, empathy, humor, and joy.

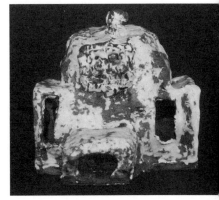

Perhaps we are all more fortunate to be part of a school where inner process-work is socially engaged; where we can get closer to the power of life as we live in a research environment; and where we learn together how to "unlimit" our practices, our beliefs, our strategies, and our selves.

Other Resources from Redleaf Press
....

Infant and Toddler Experiences
Fran Hast and Ann Hollyfield
> Filled with experiences—not activities—that promote the healthiest
> development in infants and toddlers.

More Infant and Toddler Experiences
Fran Hast and Ann Hollyfield
> Filled with over 100 engaging new ways to fill infants' and toddlers' lives
> with rich experiences that reflect and celebrate each child's development.

No Biting: Policy and Practice for Toddler Programs
Gretchen Kinnell for the Child Care Council of Onondaga County, Inc.
> The "how-to" manual for every toddler program seeking to address biting
> incidents from developmental, emotional, and practical perspectives.

Good Going! Successful Potty Training for Children in Child Care
Gretchen Kinnell for the Child Care Council of Onondaga County, Inc.
> Designed as a comprehensive approach to potty training in child care,
> *Good Going!* addresses the issues involved when children are potty trained
> in the classroom as well as in the home.

Beginning with Babies
Mary Lou Kinney and Patricia Witt Ahrens
> An easy-to-use guide containing dozens of activities to help teachers provide
> developmentally appropriate care for children from birth through fifteen months.

Prime Times: A Handbook for Excellence in Infant and Toddler Programs
Jim Greenman and Anne Stonehouse
> An essential guide to establishing a high-quality program for infants and toddlers.

Quick Quality Check for Infant and Toddler Programs
Michelle Knoll and Marion O'Brien
> *Quick Quality Check for Infant and Toddler Programs* is a quick, practical,
> and easy-to-use method for monitoring and evaluating the quality and
> consistency of care provided in infant and toddler programs. Designed for
> center and program directors.

800-423-8309
www.redleafpress.org